Stress and Anxiety Management &

Alcohol Addiction

As befitting its nature, it is presented without assurance regarding its prolonged validity or interim quality. Trademarks that are mentioned are done without written consent and can in no way be considered an endorsement from the trademark holder.

BONUS:

As promised, please use your link below to claim your 3 FREE Cookbooks on Health, Fitness & Dieting Instantly

tiny.cc/u4u27y

You can also share your link with your friends and families whom you think that can benefit from the cookbooks or you can forward them the link as a gift!

Table of Contents

Stress and Anxiety Management:

The CBT Solution for Stress Relief, Panic Attacks, and Anxiety

Chapter 1: Introduction to CBT

Cognitive Behavioral Therapy (CBT) has gained enormous popularity in recent years as a solution for anxiety, stress, and panic attacks, which largely eliminates the need for medication. Eliminating medication also eliminates the harmful side effects—and even the possibility of developing dependence.

Cognitive therapy concentrates on shifting your beliefs and patterns of thinking that are associated with or trigger stress, anxiety, or panic attacks. With CT, you're trained to understand that your beliefs produce thoughts, the thoughts produce feelings, then the feelings produce behavior. In simple terms—it's all in the mind.

You can minimize or even eliminate your stress or anxiety just by changing your perception and thinking patterns—even before the issue at hand has been dealt with. This tells you that it is possible for two people to face the same negative circumstances, wherein one remains calm and peaceful while the other is sinking in worry and anxiety. What makes the difference? It's their beliefs and thoughts.

Behavioral therapy, in particular, exposes you to your fears in a safe environment so that you can learn how to reach to those triggers. Let's say you're terrified of walking into your supervisor's office and expressing your dissatisfactions about your workplace. Begin by analyzing this fear. What is the worst that can happen? Will the supervisor turn you away or shout at you—or label you as an inciter? While all these are possibilities, they may not happen at all.

Make a plan to confront your fear. Write down exactly what you're dissatisfied with at work. Outline your points with clarity without bias. Then, book an appointment with the supervisor. If you work in a bit of a freelance environment, you can bypass the formalities and knock right at his/her door. Sit down and explain calmly why the particular issues need to be addressed—and watch the reaction.

There will definitely be sweaty moments, but you'll walk out of that office feeling empowered, celebrating your small victory of taking the first step. After that, the idea of addressing your seniors will no longer disarm you. This is just one example—you can definitely apply the same technique to your other fears and see the reaction. Oftentimes, those worst-case scenarios that you had conjured in your mind won't even happen. In the future, you can refer to that incidence when to remind yourself that worry does not solve anything—taking action does.

In general, CBT refers to a range of therapies that seek to emphasize the critical role of beliefs and self-awareness in an individual's emotions, thoughts, and actions.

What Can You Expect from Therapy Sessions?

CBT sessions, just like any other training, are time-bound. They aim to train you to get rid of retrogressive thinking and embrace more positive thoughts. Once this is achieved, mostly after about 15 sessions, you can then go and practice what you've learned.

The therapist works with you to identify the issues that are causing you stress, anxiety and/or panic attacks. How have you attempted to deal with these issues in the past? Your answer will help gauge your beliefs, perceptions, thinking, and problem-solving skills. You will then be guided on better techniques of dealing with the issues.

Benefits of CBT

1. CBT introduces your brain to a new, different, and more informed way of seeing the world and yourself. It changes you from the inside out. This is so much more than dealing with the issue at hand. In other therapies, attention is focused on the problem. Let's take an example of one dealing with divorce. Attention will be drawn to the particular incidences of divorce —tearing the memories apart to figure out what happened and how the victim felt about it, then going ahead to look for some solution. CBT takes a different approach—that of changing the perception of the victim towards the incident and creating a new way of looking at it. The victim acquires skills that can be used even in the future. In case challenges come his/her way again, they'll encounter a new person who is better prepared to cope.

2. You learn to control your thinking. Sometimes, when confronted with stress, anxiety, or panic, the brain seems to acquire a life of its own. Your thoughts get a kick of adrenalin and race about and often fail to come up with any meaningful solution. CBT teaches you to control your thinking. Just as you control your steps, deciding whether to walk slowly or run fast, so can you control your thoughts. When you have an issue at hand, you can slow down and think rationally and clearly, and this will enhance your chances of coming up with a solution and remaining calm in the process.

3. Your beliefs about yourself shift towards the positive. This life with all its ups and downs can intimidate you so that you think of yourself as weak, vulnerable, and incapable. With time, these notions become a part of you. CBT helps reaffirm you with positive thoughts, reminding you that you're strong, courageous

and capable. This boosts your confidence and places you in a better position to deal with challenges in the future.

4. Once you learn how to manage your stress, anxiety, and panic, you go through life more relaxed and calm. These emotions can wreak havoc in your life, making you a prisoner of your thoughts and tossing you around at will. By learning better practices of coping and managing them, you can look forward to more stable days ahead.

5. You learn to expect positive outcomes from life. If your past has been plagued by so many issues, you learn to expect just that. Since you attract what you think, you end up experiencing even more negative circumstances. With positive thoughts, you learn to expect pleasant things. You change your behavior to match someone expecting good things. As you believe, so are they granted unto you. In the following chapters who will learn various practices that will shift your life for the better.

Chapter 2: Decoding Stress and Anxiety

Stress and anxiety share several symptoms—so much so that the terms are often used interchangeably. Sometimes, you may not be sure what you're suffering from, as the symptoms may intertwine.

Stress occurs when the body is exposed to an external trigger and is mostly a temporary experience. Once the trigger is dealt with, the stress goes away. Stress can actually be positive in some instances. Case in point when you have a tight deadline to meet and a load of work to do, the resultant stress can give a kick of adrenalin that sees you actually compete for the work right on time. You could have sworn you would not manage that task in the given time—yet there you are.

Stress can also drive you to make a drastic decision that you previously didn't have the courage to—like when your boss makes a harsh, disrespectful comment towards you, and you find yourself drafting that resignation letter you've avoided for months.

On the other hand, which is often the case, prolonged stress is harmful to your mind and body. When the external pressure gets too much and you're struggling to cope, the negative effects begin to manifest. The pressure here could be coming from unresolved issues surrounding your job, finances, marriage, relationships, loss, family, business, and so on.

Symptoms of Stress

Emotional Symptoms

As the stress takes a toll on you, you begin to get irritable and moody. You'll be angry at anyone and anything for no particular reason. Nobody likes to be around a moody person, and those around you will avoid you at worst and tolerate you at best. If you do not confide in them what is going on, given that you may not be aware of it either, they will treat you with similar contempt making your stress even worse.

Resultant frustration will lead you to avoid others. You will steer away from social gatherings, and skip work/school at every opportunity you get. Now you lose the opportunity to talk over your issues with someone who might point you to a solution, and you end up struggling with the stress for much longer.

Stress turns your mind into a battlefield, with thoughts tossing and turning trying to find a solution. You will find that you have a hard time trying to quiet the mind. The thoughts overwhelm you and you feel like you're spinning out of control. With such negativity inside of you, you may eventually suffer from low self-esteem, often feeling weak, lonely, worthless and unattractive.

Physical Symptoms

Prolonged stress affects the body in so many ways. Headaches are some of the most common signs of the onset of a stressful period. The pain is worse at the back of the head and extends to the neck. If the conflict remains unresolved, the headaches increase in frequency and intensity. At the beginning, the common pain suppressing tablets may work—but with time you'll need stronger medication until nothing seems to work anymore.

Stress also lowers the immune system, and find yourself suffering from ailments that you've not suffered before, or at least not that frequently. You may deal with colds, stomach upsets, constipation, and even diarrhea. Coupled with the reduced energy, the opportunistic ailments only add more strain to an already tense situation.

You may experience periods of nervous sweating and shaking, especially when the trigger is close by. Your heart will beat rapidly and you'll feel all together dissolution. Clenching of the jaw is also common, mostly subconsciously, as if you're internally gathering the courage to deal with the torment in your mind.

Stress messes your libido, especially in men. Your sexual desire decreases or disappears altogether. Men may experience premature ejaculation or erectile dysfunction. If you find yourself dealing with a combination of these symptoms when facing some pressure in your life, then it is time to seek help.

Behavioral Symptoms

Stress alters your behavior in several ways. Let's start with your appetite. It can be affected, either way, so you end up overeating or undereating. If you undereat, you'll further reduce your energy levels, and you'll find yourself struggling even with the most basic of tasks. If the stress causes your cravings and hunger pangs, you're likely to overindulge, mostly in sugary and fatty fast foods in an effort to comfort yourself. Soon enough, you may be dealing with excess weight and the horde of health problems that come with it.

Sleep is also interrupted, both in quality and in quantity. While you previously slept soundly every night, you now find yourself tossing and turning in bed for hours, unable to get any restful sleep.
Your days will be colored with negativity, hardly seeing anything pleasant even in things that you previously enjoyed.

Your work also suffers since you find yourself unable to focus on a single task for a length of time. Your judgment will be clouded and you'll find it difficult to make decisions. There is the temptation to keep postponing tasks and generally avoid responsibility at all cost.

These symptoms sure look grim, but there is definitely hope at the end of the tunnel. Since stress results from a particular identifiable pressure, it can be dealt with by sorting the issue, or at least shifting your mind to that you can better accommodate the changes.

Symptoms of Anxiety

Anxiety is often a result of stress. It is a constant worry about the future, dwelling on mostly negative possibilities. While stress is worry over what is happening, anxiety is the constant worry over what could happen.

Mild anxiety is normal—you feel it at your child's first day at school, before making a presentation, when attending an interview, and so on. There is nothing wrong with this form of anxiety, and it dissipates as soon as you get over the particular task.

Anxiety becomes a concern when the worrying is constant, even when you can't tell the exact cause of the worry. Even when you're able to identify the source of uneasiness and begin to deal with it, the anxiety does not go away. It just hangs over your head reminding you that things could get worse.

Most of the symptoms of anxiety are similar to those of stress. Others are quite different and tend to last longer since anxiety does not go away as soon as the trigger is eliminated as is the case with stress.

Excess Worry

If you're suffering from anxiety, you'll worry excessively about every little thing, conjuring images of worst-case scenarios in your mind. This makes it hard to concentrate on any task as your thoughts are racing and not settling on anything in particular. This interrupts your daily life, making it difficult to interact with people or do anything meaningful.

Agitation

Are you having busts of anger even without any particular provocation? You will shout, snap at people, throw things and even then you'll not feel any better. If anything, the commotion in your mind will just increase. Unfortunately, such an attitude also drives people away from you, reducing the chances of getting the help that you need.

Restlessness and Fatigue

These two seem like a contradiction. A restless person should be moving around and attempting one task or the other. A fatigued person, on the other hand, is likely to be lying down without much energy to get anything done. How then can the 2 go together? Well, with anxiety, it actually happens. You will be restless, often pacing about and touching one chore or the other, but hardly getting anything done. You will feel tired in body and mind, unable to focus on any particular thing. At the end of the day, you'll simply be whiling your time away without getting anything meaningful done.

Muscle Tension

Anxiety causes short, shallow breaths—and as a result, you end up with inadequate oxygen in the bloodstream. This results in muscle tension. The tension feels like fatigue, especially when you've been in one position for long, like sitting in the office for hours. Eventually, tension will cause pain. You can get some temporary relief by tensing and releasing the muscles periodically.

Solitude

Anxiety drives you away from people. If you were previously social and you find yourself coming up with every excuse not to get past your door, you could be suffering from anxiety. It will fill you with worry, and paint pictures of negative scenarios that might happen if you get out there. What if people don't like you? What if they make fun of how you look? What if you attempt to speak in front of people and get embarrassed? The voices in your head will fill you will all these worries, and you'll have a hard time stepping out of the house.

Panic Attacks

A panic attack is an intense, overwhelming sensation of fear. It builds up abruptly and could be accompanied by shaking, sweating, hyperventilating, tightness of the chest, and nausea. A panic attack can make you lose control all of a sudden. To an observer, you may appear as one having a heart attack. Look out for steps to take when the attack strikes, which have been covered in a different chapter.

Even having covered these symptoms, sometimes, it is hard to tell when you're suffering from stress and anxiety. 'Isn't worrying just normal? I'm just a bit bothered by some issues, but I'm not really sick.' You may try to rationalize how you feel, just so you don't fall into the category of people who suffer from mental issues. This can be dangerous, as when left unchecked, the emotions can lead to depression.

If you're not sure of how you've been feeling or behaving lately, ask a trusted friend. Have you been avoiding occasions that you previously attended? Are there close friends that you've not spoken to for ages?

Have you exhibited any noticeable behavior change? You may have missed or justified these signals, but someone from the outside can tell.

Maybe those around you, including your family have been wondering how to approach your behavior change, but once you ask for their honest opinion, you open a channel for a discussion that could see you receive the help that you need.

Get into the habit of journaling. When you feel like you can't talk to anyone, put it down. Writing eliminates the element of being judged. It also holds your secrets for you, issues that you would not be comfortable telling to anyone else.

Reading your own journal can lead to a self-diagnosis. Look at your thought patterns and your behavior over a period of time, and establish a pattern which will inform what about you has changed. If you notice a negative change, it is definitely a cause of concern.

You can also speak to a specialist who is well versed with the matters of stress and anxiety. A therapist will pick cues even from those small things that you may ignore. Most people avoid speaking to a counselor as they don't want to feel interrogated, or have their privacy intruded. They're pleasantly surprised to find that therapists ask you gentle leading questions and you find yourself opening up on your own volition.

Experiencing stress and anxiety is not new. The point is to make an effort to manage them and keep them at bay whenever possible. Whether you're already suffering from the conditions or you're reading this book as a prevention measure, you will find plenty of techniques to guide you.

Chapter 3: Coping with Stress

Positive Ways of Coping with Stress

Identify the Source of Stress

Can you pinpoint what is causing you strain? Sometimes, the source is straightforward—such as a failed relationship, divorce, unpleasant job, bills, and so on. In other instances, you can't really tell what is causing the tension—at least not until you think about it critically. Sometimes, stress creeps up on you slowly but steadily, such that by the time you notice the tension, you can't really tell when it started.

If you're in this second group, this one is for you. Analyze your situation with the aim of establishing the pattern of your stress. How long have you been unhappy? If you can't figure that out, then ask— when is the last time I was really happy? It could be months or even years ago. What changed that? When did the joy and contentment begin to subside?

Often, you'll realize that a good situation started gradually going south, and the strain set in bit by bit and almost caught you unawares. You could have been in a happy marriage, the things slowly shifted. You could have been content with your job, then with time it demanded more and more of your time. You could have been doing well financially, but expenses increased as your kids progressed in school. Such slow changes increase your stress bit by bit until you can hardly tell when it started. Once you analyze your situation and determine the source of the stress, you'll be one step ahead in managing it.

What Needs to Change?

Once you've identified your source of stress, determine what needs to change, and find the courage to initiate that change. We often wallow in discomfort simply because it's familiar. Determine to overcome the fear of change and usher yourself to a better place.

If you have a stressful job, speak to your boss about adjusting your working conditions. If things don't seem to get better, you may as well consider opting out of the job. You can find a job with better terms, or start your own business.

The same applies to relationships. If holding on is causing you more pain than letting go, perhaps it's time to call it a day. The strain of a relationship that's not working is worse than being alone. Take that time to reconnect with yourself, and remind yourself of your goals, dreams, vision, and purpose in life. You should move to the next relationship with clarity, knowing exactly what you expect to give and receive.

If your finances are the issue, then you need to find extra income streams. Take a second job. Arrange for your spouse to work as well. Explore ways of working online. If no extra money is forthcoming, then consider cutting downgrading your expenditure.

These are just some examples of the changes that you can make. Determine the adjustment you need to make according to your individual circumstances. Being bold enough to make the change leaves you feeling empowered—a good place to start your journey to a stress-free life.

Unwind Daily

Every day comes with its own challenges. These matters strain your mind, heart, and body and if left to build up will result in stress. Find something pleasant and relaxing to do at the end of the day to distract your mind from the issues you're going through. Revive an old hobby. Or get a new one. Set aside time each day to engage in that one activity that gives you so much joy that you hardly feel the time pass. It could be watching a movie/documentary/sport, listening to good music, reading, cooking, sewing, drawing, painting, meditating, gardening, cycling, and so on.

Take the activity a notch higher by setting a target. You can decide, for instance, to read one book every week. Or learn a new drawing/painting technique in 10 days. Or cycle for 2 kilometers every day. How about you grow a new set of vegetables/flowers in the next month?

Setting a goal shifts your energy. You're now preoccupied in strategizing on how to achieve the goal. Join a community of fellow enthusiast. It could be in your neighborhood or even online. This opens you to a whole new level—engage with others, exchange tips, hold each other accountable, grow your skill, take part in competitions, and possibly make lifelong friends. No matter what else is going on in your life, you will always have something to look forward to.

Prioritize You

No matter how crazy things feel around you, make time for yourself. Exercise. Choose a form of physical exercise that you enjoy. You can walk, jog, run, cycle, swim, do aerobics, and so on. Make it outdoors whenever possible, the sights and sounds of nature are therapy in themselves. When indoors, pop in some music and dance, vigorously sometimes, till you break into a sweat.

Eat healthy, balanced meals. Cut down on processed fast foods opting for fresh food. Stress can take away your energy, and wholesome, nutritious food is just what you need to keep you nourished. Healthy food also keeps you away from the disease. You definitely don't want to aggravate whatever is troubling you with ill health. In case you're already struggling with one health issue or another, healthy eating will help you better manage the condition and enhance your peace of body and mind.

Get adequate sleep—in quality and quantity. You can be in bed for 8 hours, yet the better part of that time is spent tossing and turning battling the thoughts in your mind. Once stress disrupts your sleep, you'll spend the following day fatigued and hardly able to execute any meaningful task. That only adds to the stress, right? Then the stress keeps you from sleeping yet again, and the downward spiral just continues. Induce sleep with whatever works for you—reading, music, a relaxing bath, and so on. After a good rest, you'll be alert and better placed to deal with the matters causing you stress.

You don't have to let what you're feeling reflect on the outside. Be mindful of your hygiene and grooming. Get a new haircut. Add some new pieces to your wardrobe. Get a message. Or a facial treatment. Glow from the outside. Once you like what you see in the mirror, you'll be more confident to go out there and make things happen.

Manage Your Time

If you feel like you're always running around with tonnes of things to do, you need to make some changes around here as well. Are you spending too much time at work with hardly any time for anything else? Perhaps you need to explore more efficient ways of getting the job done so you don't have to take so long. There could be a software or an App that can get the job done faster. Delegating is also an option. How about you work from home sometimes so you can utilize the time otherwise spent in traffic?

As for the other tasks, make a to-do list for the week and break it into daily activities. Start your days early so you can get more done. There are those tasks that only you can do. Like attending the parents meeting at your child's school. Others, like shopping, you can delegate. You don't have to do everything, really. Outsource what can be done by others. Utilize online services. Let your family members chip in and help. Otherwise, you'll be running around every day, yet you'll hardly have time to spend on yourself.

Learn to say no. You don't have to feel guilty about setting limits. Sometimes, you just have enough on your hands, and you have to respectfully say no to other invitations. You can't be everywhere. You can't please everybody. This might upset some acquaintances, but such is life.

Talk to Somebody

A problem shared with the right ear is really a problem half solved. You do not have to battle your issues all alone. Speaking out in itself is therapeutic—you feel lighter even before you start discussing the possible options. You also get to listen to yourself outline the problem. It is possible to battle an issue in your mind for so long, yet never speak it out. Just saying it out loud gives you some clarity.

Speak to a friend, family member, colleague or acquaintance. Stress clouds your judgment and reasoning, making it even more difficult to find solutions for the stressors. Somebody else listening to you and examining the situation critically is better placed to help you find a way out.

If you prefer to speak to a stranger, there are professional counselors online and offline. They are trained to deal with diverse personalities on a wide range of matters and suggest possible paths that will lead you out of the stress. This is a good option when you want your information to remain confidential.

Remember, ultimately, the answer lies with you. Those you speak to can only direct and encourage you, but the journey is yours to take.

Form Meaningful Relationships

As we have discussed above, you may be one of those people who feel like you have no one to talk to even though you have company. There are people around you, yet you don't feel connected enough to any of them to share your issues.

This age of social media has made our relationships fickle. You spend hours online interacting with all manner of people, yet none of them are close to you. To make matters worse, people only bring the best illusion of themselves on social media—floss mode, basically. Everyone seems to be making it. You browse through tonnes of glossy pictures of your peers in seemingly great jobs, posh houses and cars, picture-perfect relationships, and so on. Then you look at your life, at the issues plaguing you, and you feel like you're at the bottom of the pack.

Beyond the surface, most of those people are battling issues just like you. They're mostly just putting up appearances for the Gram, as many of us do. You don't have to stomach this social media pressure to measure up. Remember we talked about making changes? This could be one of the drastic changes that you need to make.

Suspend or even deactivate your social media accounts. Get offline and reconnect with your family, friends, neighbors, colleagues, and acquaintances. Talk and listen to them. Get to know their personalities, dreams, philosophies, hobbies, pains, and so on even as you express yours. Let them become your support system even as you become part of theirs. Sharing constantly with people who truly care about you will definitely reduce your stress.

Negative Ways of Coping with Stress

Alcohol/Drugs

These will stimulate you only for a short while, then the effect will wear off, leaving you not only with your issues but also with the side effects. You will be exposed to diseases, addiction, withdrawal symptoms, and so on that will only aggravate the situation.

Over/Undereating

Different people react differently to stress. Some will eat and eat—others will hardly take a bite. Overeating will likely result in excess weight and the health issues that come with it. Undereating will starve you of the energy you need to attend to your everyday life—let alone deal with your stress.

Oversleeping

There are those who will spend their days in bed, curtains drawn, barely differentiating between day and night. What does that solve? Nothing! Running away from your issues to slumber-land will not move them, they'll be still there when you finally roll out of bed.

Overindulgence

We talked of hobbies as a way of dealing with stress, but if you overindulge, that too is a problem. You can watch movies, or play video games, but definitely not all day. The point is to give you a positive distraction for some time, not to turn you into a couch potato. Eventually, you must make an effort to leave that comfort zone and go attend to the matters that are causing you stress.

Chapter 4: Anxiety Relief and Management

Master Your Thoughts

Anxiety is all in your mind, dwelling on perceived negative outcomes of various situations. When the worry comes, you can let it pass without harming you. As someone put it, "Keep the front and back door open. Let the worries come and go. Just don't serve them tea." Don't dwell on them. Think of them as the clouds floating by—you see them one moment, and the next they've passed.

Should the anxiety persist, you can shift the negative thoughts to positive ones. Remember your thoughts ultimately affect your behavior. If you think nobody likes you at your workplace, you'll act like it. You'll isolate yourself, skip work-related events and miss work at every given opportunity. Ultimately, your performance will suffer.

What if you told yourself that you're competent at your job and an asset to the company? Your actions will be guided by that notion. You'll come to work on time. You'll work with vigor, and make an effort to relate well with your colleagues. Once you shift your thoughts from negative to positive, it trickles down to everything else that you do.

Identify the Underlying Issues

What really is causing your anxiety? Think about it critically. The issues could be related to your job, finances, marriage, relationships, health, and so on. Is there something you can do to make the situation better? Well, take action. Taking even a small step towards finding the solution is empowering and gives you that push that you need to face your worries.

If you're unhappy in your job, speak to a career counselor, albeit online. Explore your options. Can you get a better position at your workplace? Can you delegate some tasks that you feel are not suited for you? Can you look for another job? Or start your own business? How about you go back to school and acquire more skills to make you more marketable? Brainstorm. Weigh your options—the pros and cons of each one. As you begin to take action, clarity replaces the anxiety.

Identify the Triggers

Is your anxiety accelerated by a certain sight, sound or memory? Identify the triggers so you can avoid them, or at least know how to react to them. Let's say you're embroiled in a children custody battle after a divorce. Every time you see an email or a missed call from the lawyer, anxiety descends on you. What if I lose my children? What if I'll be required to pay hefty child support fees? Well, that could be the case; or not. This is an issue you have to face. You cannot escape it. You can only devise ways of dealing with this particular trigger. For instance, you can instruct the lawyer that all communication is to be done on a certain day of the week, say Saturday. You then spend that day dwelling on that issue, then you know you have a whole week of peace before the next session.

Some triggers can be avoided. If driving on a certain road makes you anxious due to a certain accident, you can use an alternative route. Or let somebody else drive.

Once you're familiar with the triggers, you will respond accordingly and avoid being overwhelmed by anxiety.

Divert Your Attention to Something You Enjoy

A positive distraction works fast to calm your mind. Listen to music, watch a movie, read a book, draw, paint, knit, cook, garden, dance, play an instrument or do whatever else makes you happy.

If such activity offers physical exercise, it'll be twice as helpful. An active body produces the feel-good hormone endorphin, which makes you feel happy, refreshed, relaxed and improves your general well-being. Chose a form of exercise that you enjoy and look forward to. It can be walking, jogging, running, cycling, swimming, aerobics, yoga, and so on.

Exercise outdoors whenever you can. The healing power of nature never grows old. Feel the breeze in your hair, the warmth of the sun and the musky smell of than earth. Bring a dash of nature in our house by keeping potted plants. Open the windows—let the wind and sunshine in. As you let your senses soak in nature, the anxiety will only be a distant feeling.

Get Enough Sleep

If the anxiety keeps you awake at night, as it often does, it will only compound the condition by adding fatigue to it. Try to establish a schedule. Research shows that you sleep better when you go to bed at the same time every night. You can have an evening schedule like exercise, dinner, shower and sleep in that order every day.

Mind the quality as well as the quantity of sleep. 8 hours of deep sleep is recommended. If you're in bed tossing and turning and listening to the noise in your mind, that hardly counts as meaningful sleep. You'll wake up still tired, then the day ahead will be rough on your mind and body, leading to even more anxiety.

In addition to the fixed schedule, you can induce sleep with music, reading, a bubble bath, dimming of lights or whatever else works for you. A rested mind faces a new day with clarity and keeps anxiety at bay.

Take the Focus Off Yourself

Step out of your comfort zone and be of assistance to somebody else. Take part in community improvement initiatives. Volunteer at a shelter for the homeless, children's orphanage or a home for the aged. Out there you'll interact with people whose situations are so much worse, and you'll look at your issues and they'll seem to shrink.

So many people out there are having it worse. Are you behind on rent? Well, at least you have a house. Are you going through a divorce? At least you got a chance to love and be loved in return. Some have never had such a special relationship. Are you having a hard time at your workplace? At least you have a job.

Making time for the less fortunate in society reminds you of how much you really have. Instead of worrying over what may happen in the future, you now count your blessings and can't help but be grateful for all that life has given to you.

Improve Your Self-Esteem

Social anxiety often comes from a place of not feeling good enough. You end up avoiding people and social gatherings. Ask yourself some candid questions about your fears. What's the worst that could happen? What exactly are you afraid of?

Picture yourself starting a conversation with your school-mates or colleagues. Are you afraid of expressing yourself poorly and not being understood? Then work on your communication. Are you afraid that you'll have nothing important to say? Then work on your content, so that you're well versed with relevant information. Remember there's a possibility that there's nothing wrong with you and the manner in which you communicate—the inadequacies are all just imagined. Put yourself out there and let the reception guide you on how to proceed.

Make an effort to be presentable. Mind your hygiene and grooming. Dress for the occasion. Get some new outfits. Or a new hairstyle.

Anything that boosts your confidence reduces your social anxiety and allows you to have meaningful interactions with those around you.

Learn Relaxation Practices

There are simple things that you can do to keep you calm in the face of a wave of anxiety. Taking deep breaths is the simplest of them all, and you can do it anywhere. Slow down your breathing, taking time to inhale, hold the breath then exhale just as slowly. Within a few breaths, you will begin to feel your muscles relax and heartbeat stabilize as more oxygen flows through your bloodstream.

Close your eyes, especially if your immediate environment is worsening the anxiety. Picture yourself in a tranquil, pleasant place such as a picnic site. Think about how each of your senses would be taking in the scenes. Imagine yourself seated on the grass next to your picnic basket, surrounded by the greenery, clouds floating above. Imagine hearing the birds chirping. And the scent of fresh sandwiches coming from your basket. Picture yourself lying there, head propped on a pillow, reading your favorite novel. Now open your eyes. Viola! The anxious moment has passed.

Anxiety often causes muscle tension. Relax your muscles by tensing then releasing a group of muscles at a time. Start with your feet and travel all the way up. With time, you'll learn to identify the onset of muscle tension and do the necessary in good time.

Yoga, meditation, music therapy and aromatherapy are also relaxation techniques that you can use to get you through that anxious moment. The details have been expounded in another chapter. Experiment with the relaxation techniques to find out what works best for you.

Counseling

When those constant episodes of anxiety are left unattended, they can develop into chronic anxiety which becomes a permanent feature of your life, often leading to other health conditions. A professional counselor can help you identify the source of your anxiety, recognize the triggers and take appropriate steps to alleviate the condition.

There is the option of talking to a friend or a family member, but that tends to be a one-time conversation. There will be an emotional talk, tears, pats on the back, hugs, and that's it.

Speaking to a professional ensures there's follow up. There will be formal sessions where you'll speak of your fears and worries. The therapist will help you deconstruct them, and separate those that you can change from those that you cannot do anything about. Is your worry based on something that you can change? Well, then begin to take action. If it's something you can't change, then works towards accepting and adjusting to it.

Mindfulness

Resist the urge to antagonize about the future, instead focusing on the present. Take time to notice your surroundings. For instance, if you're in your house, look at the arrangement of your furniture. How about you rearrange the pieces for a new look? Begin to reposition them in your mind. Can the book cabinet fit in that corner? How about moving the couch closer to the window? And those cushions could do with a different color.

Listen to the sound of music from the stereo. Try to guess the instruments being played. How about those scents coming from the kitchen? What spices could those be? Allow your mind to be consumed by what is right there in front of you. Not what could happen, but what is happening, and here anxiety has no room.

Join a Support Group

The wearer of the shoe knows where it pinches, right? Those who suffer from anxiety stand the best chance of understanding what you're going through. Some who have not experienced constant anxiety do not understand that it's actually a condition. They wonder why you can't simply snap out of it. Unable to explain, you'll most likely retreat to your cocoon and continue battling the worries plaguing your mind.

In a support group, you'll be right at home. You'll listen to others describe their experiences, and sometimes, you'll feel like they're expounding your exact situation. Once you realize that you're not alone, you'll find it easier to open up. You can then exchange ideas, coping mechanisms, remedies, and so on. Here you can also make friends that will always stand by you in your hour of need.

Avoid the temptation to go for the quick fix. Alcohol, drugs, and caffeine may give you some immediate relief, but it is only temporary and will, in the long run, aggravate the situation. Aim for slow but sure progress where you deal fundamentally with your perceptions and thoughts, and the positive effects will eventually trickle down to your mind. Anxiety does not have to take over your life; you can manage it and go on with your life uninterrupted.

Chapter 5: Reset your Anxious Mind

Permit the Worry

The first instance an anxious thought crosses your mind, you may try to block it, thus causing even more anxiety. Give it time—just not too much. In fact, some experts suggest that you should schedule a "worry time" where you actually think critically of what is troubling you.

For instance, if you're behind on bills, look critically at your finances. Look at your income and expenditure. Are you spending more than you're earning? Can you earn more at your current job maybe by working overtime or taking on extra tasks? Can you get a second job? Can you get some online jobs that you can do during your free time? If you can't earn more money at the moment, then reduce your expenditure. Cut out the non-essentials. Plan on how to clear your bills —which one to begin with, how much to pay every month, and so on.

See? You have used your 'worry time' to come up with something constructive—a plan. Now every time this particular worry begins to float in your head, remind yourself that you have a plan.

Apply the same 'worry time' to other matters. Mostly, you'll be worrying over stuff that has not happened yet—or has no certainty of happening—yet you'll find yourself burdening your mind with "what if?" Like in the case above, you'll be wondering: what if I can't pay rent and I'm kicked out of my house? What if I hit my credit card limit? What if I can't afford even the necessities?

Once again, remind yourself that you have a plan. Steer your thoughts towards the positive. 'I will pay all my bills on time. I will earn more. I will pay my credit card debts.' After the 'worry time' comes a period of clarity and calm.

Journal

At that moment when anxiety seems to be taking over your mind, write down exactly what you're feeling. You probably have a notepad on your phone—bypass that and go for a physical notebook. There is power in holding the pen and letting the ink run on a page.

Writing gives you the impression of unloading the mind. Unlike talking to someone where you might be afraid to mention some things, here, you can unload everything. You'll feel the burden ease with every sentence.

Once the anxious moments have passed, you can revisit what you wrote and analyze it. Often, you'll realize that the situation is not as bad as it felt. What is causing you all that worry is more perception than reality. You will also establish the trigger of the anxiety and be more prepared to face it the next time.

Live in the Moment

Anxiety is basically thinking about the future, and what could happen. Every time your mind attempts to travel ahead to that uncertain future, draw it back to the present. Notice your surroundings. The sights, sounds, and scents. If you're in a familiar environment that has nothing new to offer, step out. The outdoors works great in such moments.

Let your senses be alert. Take time to notice the things that you've never noticed before. Look at the trees, the shadows, the sky. Listen to the chirping birds. Inhale the musky smell of the earth. As your senses soak at the moment, the anxiety will have been relegated to a distance.

Distract Yourself

Turn your attention to something that you enjoy. Maybe a pop of music is all you need to dab the anxiety away. Music is a real healer, and you can listen to it anywhere. Put together uplifting and inspirational songs in your phone or iPod. With earphones, you can play music anywhere.

Get a hobby or revive an old one so you can always have something to switch to when the battle seems to be having the better of your mind. Watch TV, read a book, draw, paint, cook, meditate, or do anything else that you find pleasant. Don't overindulge though. Remember the activity is only supposed to give you a positive distraction for some moments. Don't use it as an escape route and ignore the source of your anxiety. Let it give you a moment of joy so you can come back with clarity.

Positive Thoughts

Anxiety dwells on the possibility of bad things happening—but the opposite is also true, right? What if the test comes back positive for a disease? Well, what if it comes back negative? What if my business fails? How about if it actually thrives? Whenever your mind slides towards negative possibilities, steer it towards positive possibilities.

And should negative things occur anyway, like they do every once in a while, you can handle them. Reaffirm yourself. Remind yourself that you're strong, resilient and capable. You have gone through storms before and made it out in one piece. Anxiety and positive thoughts hardly ever dwell together—soon enough, you'll regain your calm and peace of mind.

Just Do It

If you're anxious about a certain activity, you may as well get it over with. Make that phone call that you've been postponing for days. Knock on your boss's door to express your concern on various work issues. Talk to your partner about those suspicious text messages you came across some weeks ago. Hand in that resignation letter. What's the worst that could happen?

You'll never know until you actually attempt it. Your mind may be conjuring all sorts of worst-case scenarios, but things may not end up that bad. In fact, the empowering feeling of doing what you had been afraid of is just what you need to get rid of the anxiety.

Once in a while, when the anxiety strikes, sit back and have a blank moment. Do absolutely nothing. Just sit comfortably and take deep breaths. Let the moment pass, then shift your attention to your usual activities. Anxiety often feels like a commotion going on in your mind, and these tips should help you quiet all that noise so you can regain your peace.

Chapter 6: Reset Your Body for Optimum Health

The strain exerted on the body by everyday activities upsets its natural equilibrium and leaves if offset. It is in this offset state that you experience fatigue, stress, anxiety, and even increases the chances of other health issues.

Just as you reset a machine once in a while so it can perform optimally, your body should be reset periodically as well. The main areas involved in resetting the body includes sleep, hormones, and metabolism.

Sleep

Your sleep pattern follows the internal clock, also known as the circadian clock. This is a mechanism that delivers signals to the body when it's time to sleep and time to wake up. Most of us go to bed at around 10 pm and wake up at 6 am or so. You will notice that whenever this sleeping time approaches, you'll begin to feel drowsy. Then in the morning, you will wake up at about the same time even without an alarm clock.

The body loves and thrives in routine. If this sleep routine is disrupted, the body will voice a complaint in one way or the other. You'll feel tired during the day, or at least the better part of the day, then be awake at night. This disrupts your energy and makes you less productive.

Sleep disruptors could be external, such as lighting and temperature. Similarly, they can be internal such as genetics and hormones. Changing your habits also changes your sleeping pattern, such as when you nap during the day or change your eating hours. Travelling, especially when you cross to different time zones, is also a major factor affecting sleeping patterns.

Here are some tips that you can employ to reset your sleep:

1. Manipulate your indoor lighting. The body is used to responding to natural lighting. If you lie down in a dim room during the day, chances are you'll begin to feel drowsy. On the other hand, if the room has a bright light at night, you'll have a hard time falling asleep. This technique is especially important when dealing with jet lag or a similar feeling. Jet lag is that sluggish feeling that you feel when you've flown across time zones.

   For instance, you leave one region in the morning, fly for about 9 hours, and you're expecting to arrive in the evening so you can lay down to rest. However, your destination happens to be in a different time zone, so instead of arriving in the evening, you arrive in another morning. Your body, having been used to a schedule, gets confused. There you are trying to catch some sleep, yet it is high noon, with the sun shining brightly. Perhaps by the time your body gets used to that time zone, you travel back, and the process is repeated all over again. Train your body to get back to your regular sleeping pattern by adjusting the lighting.

2. Try to stick to a regular sleeping schedule. Sleep and wake up at the same time every day. If you keep sleeping and waking at different hours, you send the body to offset. If you're having trouble falling asleep, try to induce sleep by playing soft background music, reading or anything else that works for you. Avoid stimulants such as caffeine before bedtime. Keep away

from electronics as well—TV, phone, and video games keep you alert instead of inducing sleep.

3. Manage stress and anxiety, as they affect the quality and quantity of sleep. The worries in your mind keep you turning and tossing for hours without getting any meaningful sleep. The lack of sleep further aggravates the conditions, and it's a downward spiral from there. Find relaxing ways of inducing sleep. Resist the temptation to always reach out for sleeping pills. They will work at first, but with time you'll be required to increase the dosage, and eventually, you could be dependent on the pills, always needing them to be able to sleep. Such frequent medication also exposes you to harmful side effects which can result in other health conditions. CBT, whose techniques are outlined in this book, is a sure start to manage your stress.

Metabolism

This is another crucial factor for your well-being. Metabolism is all about the food we eat and how it is digested and utilized. You can start off by fasting for a set period—that's right, start your eating plan by not eating. The point here is to clear your stomach so you can start on a clean slate, literally. Techniques such as intermittent fasting can help you start off.

After that, kick start your metabolism by selecting carefully what you eat. Healthy eating is important for all, but even more important as you grow older. Go for wholesome meals with whole grains, fiber, lean proteins, complex carbs, vegetables, and fruits. Limit processed foods and fast foods, instead opting for fresh options. Stay hydrated as well—the importance of water cannot be overemphasized.

Stress and anxiety affect your eating too. You end up eating too little or too much. Insufficient food robs you of your energy. Too much food leads to excess weight which exposes you to a whole new realm of discomposure and possible diseases.

Hormones

Your hormones control a good number of your bodily functions such as metabolism, emotions, libido, growth, and reproduction. Here are some steps to help you reset your hormones:

- Reduce the intake of simple carbs and sugars. They often lead to a sugar rush, which then disrupts the hormones.
- Reduce the intake of chemicals by opting for fresh food as opposed to those ridden with sweeteners and preservatives.
- Mind the quality and quantity of your sleep, aiming for 8 restful ours every night. This gives the cells time to rejuvenate and heal, enhancing the secretion of hormones.
- Protect your immune system by avoiding unhealthy food.
- Regulate the intake of medication as it introduces chemicals in the body which alter the hormones.

Regulating your sleep, hormones and metabolism go a long way in ensuring that your body is operating at its optimum.

Chapter 7: Overcome Panic and Worry

Worry is that feeling of uneasiness that grips you when you think of the troubles in your life and what they may lead to in the future. You may also worry about things that you assume could happen. Whether they end up happening or not, those moments of worry have already stolen your joy and peace and have not solved anything. The worry might be related to matters of health, finances, marriage, relationships, job, business, social pressures, and so on. Whichever the case, worry hardly helps. Below are some of the steps that you can take to overcome worry:

Examine the Worry

What are you worried about? Is it something you can change? If you can do something about the situation, then take that step. If you're worried about the status of your marriage, schedule some time to talk it over with your spouse. Read about marriages and relationships. Speak to a counselor, whether alone or with your husband/wife. As you begin to make an effort to address the issue, the worry subsides. Make a plan on how to cope or get out of the situation. Every time a worry crosses your mind after that, remind yourself that you have a plan in place, and you're working towards sorting the issue.

Communicate

We worry so often wondering what is on someone else's mind. Is my partner dissatisfied with our relationship? Is the boss unhappy with my performance at work? My parents seem unhappy with the decisions I've been making lately. We toss and turn, making assumptions about what is on other people's mind about us.

Have you thought of cutting the chase and just asking? Voice out your concerns, instead of leaving them to torment your mind to no end.

Discuss your relationship, your job or your decisions with those you've been worrying about. Often, you'll realize that you were just worrying for no reason. And should it be the case that these people actually harbor particular thoughts about you, then you'll discuss them and eliminate the doubts.

Additionally, keep in mind that people may not be thinking about you as much as you think. Really. People have tonnes of things to do, and their own lives to run. You might be worrying yourself sick wondering what they think of you, only to discover that they actually don't.

Keep Busy

It is said that worrying is like a rocking-chair activity but with no progress. Instead of dwelling on a worry, find something to keep your hands busy. If you don't have a job yet, you can volunteer. Or take up a hobby. Anything to offer some positive distraction, and perhaps achieve something constructive while at it.

Aim for small wins. Even though you don't have a job, you can take time to draft and design an exquisite resume. Or write a business plan. Or even clean, declutter and rearrange the house. Worry is fickle. As soon as you shift your attention to something else, it fades away.

Ignored worry can get so intense that it turns into panic, which is an abrupt uncontrollable fear or anxiety. Sometimes, it can develop into a full blown panic attack which involves sudden intense fear that washes over you within minutes. At that instance, you'll be trembling, sweating, and struggling to breathe. Your heart will be pounding and you'll have a hard time getting a hold of yourself. Here are some steps that you can follow if you find yourself in the middle of a panic attack:

1. Recognize that you're having a panic attack, which can be confused for a heart attack by an external eye. Should people rush up to you to help, make an effort to let them know that you're dealing with a panic attack, so they can offer you the right kind of help. Remember just as it comes swiftly, it goes away just as fast. That should give you some courage to hang on in there until the moment passes.

2. Breathe deeply, letting air fill your chest, holding for a couple of seconds then breathing out. It may seem like a lot to master in the heat of the moment, but try to make an effort. Remember the attack comes with hyperventilation, where you take in short, shallow breaths. This deprives your body of oxygen, and your muscles begin to tighten. Muscle tension is the last thing you need when your body is in that moment of weakness. Deep breathing ensures that you regain calm quickly.

3. Should you be in public where all sorts of things are happening at once, or there's a particular visual trigger, close your eyes. Try to picture yourself in a safe familiar place, such as in your house or office. Envision how that place looks like, and engage your senses so that you get the sensation of seeing and hearing what is happening there. This will bring some reprieve to your mind, and the attack will subside.

4. If you're indoors or in a safer place, look at a particular object and focus all your attention on it. Let's say that you just suffered a panic attack at your desk in the office. Immediately shift your attention to the nearby flowerpot. Look at the colors, the shapes, and contours. The aim here is to focus your mind which has been scattered by the attack. Once you distract your mind, the anxious moment loses its intensity and soon passes away.

5. Once the moment has passed try to identify the trigger so you can be prepared to deal with it the next time. Look at a series of panic attacks and see if you can identify a pattern. What did you see, hear or smell immediately before the attack? You can either choose to avoid it or to change your way of thinking so that it is no longer seen as a threat.

Next time you find yourself worrying and panicking, you now know which steps you can take to ease your mind.

Chapter 8: Relaxation Techniques to Induce Calm

Relaxation techniques come in handy in the management of stress, anxiety, and panic attacks. These techniques are easy and have minimal requirements, which gives you the freedom to do them almost anywhere and at any time. There is also the option of combining 2 or more techniques for that extra effect. As long as you can find a quiet room where you can sit comfortably, then you're all set for a relaxation technique of your choice.

Deep Breathing

Simple yet powerful, deep breathing offers instant relief to a troubled mind. A surge of anxiety or panic causes you to take quick, shallow gasps of air. This reduces the supply of oxygen in your bloodstream causing muscle tension. The deep breathing relaxation technique aims to draw more air into your body which slows down the heart rate, stabilizes the blood pressure, and relaxes the muscles.

Take a long, slow breath commonly referred to as belly or abdominal breathing. Let the air fill your chest and belly, hold for a couple of seconds, then breathe out. As you concentrate on your breathing, the anxious thoughts gradually leave.

Progressive Muscle Relaxation

This technique helps you identify muscle tension and deal with it. You focus on one muscle group at a time. Start with something as simple as the fist. Tighten your fist for a couple of seconds then release, repeating as necessary. Your hand should feel lighter and more relaxed.

Repeat the same for your feet, thighs, shoulders, and so on. Take the neck as far as it can go on each side. Feel the difference? As the tension melts away from your muscles, your mind feels calmer. With time, you'll be in a position to identify muscle tension as soon as it sets in and act accordingly.

Visualization

Imagine yourself in a beautiful, relaxing and calm place, whether real or just a figment of your imagination. Close your eyes and picture yourself lying on the beach, for instance. Let all your senses come to life. What do you see, hear, smell or touch?

Think of the expanse of blue water stretching as far as your eyes can see. Think of the sound of the crashing waves. Smell the mix of the sea water and the enticing aroma of food coming from the restaurant nearby. Feel your bare feet sink into the sand, and your body absorbing the warmth of the sun. Such a vivid visualization lets your mind and body experience the sensation of being in a different place where worry and anxiety is the last thing on your mind.

Yoga

Yoga is great for the body and mind. The twists and turns involved help release endorphins—the same feel-good hormones that are released during physical exercise. The hormones leave you feeling more stable, happier and more energetic.

Yoga is a gentle, low-intensity activity that you can engage in without straining, even when you're feeling low. You can also incorporate other relaxing techniques into yoga, such as deep breathing and meditation which we look at next.

Meditation

Meditation is related to Yoga but has less movement. You basically sit comfortably, preferably with your legs crossed and your arms folded so that your wrists rest on the knees. Much like the basic yoga pose.

Try the triangle breathing where you inhale, count let's say to 3, hold, count to 3 then exhale with a similar margin. Increase the count gradually to the number you're comfortable with. As you breathe deeply, imagine a wave of relaxation moving through you. You can add an affirming chant to your meditation. Say something positive and empowering such as 'I am healthy and whole. I am courageous. I can overcome this'. The words of affirmation will seep into your system further erasing your worry and anxiety.

Music Therapy

Music, the right kind of music, has an instant calming effect on the body and mind. Fortunately, you can carry music anywhere. Collect inspirational and uplifting music and have it close. Every time you feel stressed, worried or panicked, you can pop in a tune and soak in the beautiful words and melodies.

You do not even have to wait for your mind to be troubled in order to play music. Play it the first thing in the morning so you can start your day on a high note. Play in the car as you sit in traffic. You can even have soft music in the background at your workplace if that is allowed. Take full advantage of this readily available relaxation technique to calm your mind.

Aromatherapy

A beautiful scent has an instant uplifting effect on your mood. Scents from sources such as lavender, jojoba, lemongrass, chamomile, and rosewater are mostly used in aromatherapy. They can be packaged in different forms such as candles, body wash, air freshener, perfume or incense.

All these options are available in the market. Choose what works for you—different scents appeal to different people. Get it in a compact form that you can carry anywhere. Again, you do not have to wait for the worry to strike. You can have your scent of choice around you all day to keep your mood up. Should the anxiety strike anyway, inhale the scent deeply and repeat as necessary, and enjoy the feeling of calm that washes over you.

Examine these techniques and select what works for you. You can experiment from one to the other until you identify the one that best induces calm for you. Moreover, consider your environment so that you can evaluate which technique can be accommodated comfortably.

Do not worry if the effect is not as fast as you'd like. What works like magic for one person may not work for the other. Keep trying and exploring. If anyone cannot seem to work effectively, try different combinations as well. Then you'll no longer have to be worried about battling constant worry, your fix will just be an arm's length away.

Chapter 9: Moving Past Pain and Tragedy

Have you gone through negative experiences in the past that you can't seem to let go of? The experiences here can range from loss of a loved one, rejection, broken agreement, relationship breakup, unresolved conflict, childhood ordeals, rape, divorce, miscarriage, and so on. Such tragedies can leave deep physical and psychological wounds that take deliberate effort to heal.

How do you know that you've not healed from the hurt? Chances are that you feel numb whenever you think of the incident. Your body is trying to cope by shutting out related thoughts. You can also feel disconnected from people and from reality. You are paranoid and develop a distrust for people around you—even when they mean no harm. How can you move past this?

Accept

Why did it happen to me? What did I do wrong? What do bad things happen to good people? You must have asked yourself these questions a dozen times. Sadly, nobody has the answers. The best you can do is accept that you were a victim of unfortunate circumstances—and no, not because you did anything wrong. You're not being punished. These things happen.

Accepting keeps you from living in denial. As long as you're asking these questions, you're fleeting with the idea that the occurrence did not actually happen—like you might snap out of the daze to find that things have gone back to normal—or that the incident can actually "un-happen."

Say after a miscarriage, you keep hoping that you'll wake up and find yourself pregnant again. Or after an accident that left you on a wheelchair, part of you still anticipates that the scars will somehow disappear overnight and you'll walk again.

Such thoughts will give you some temporary comfort but are really not helpful at all. They only keep you from pursuing true healing.

Remember it is possible to be hurting without actually acknowledging it. You may be involved in alcohol and drugs, and just call it having fun. Or you're a loner who avoids interacting with people, and you'll simply say you're an introvert. Yet, beyond the surface, you're dealing with pain from your past, which is leading your actions.

Speak It Out

Those dealing with trauma tend to avoid people, mostly because they don't want to talk about the particular issue. Talking helps you accept it, which is exactly what you need. Speaking out takes courage, especially if you've buried the memories of the incident for a long time. You may stammer, cry, break down—but this is actually a positive sign of the beginning of healing.

It helps to talk to a friend or family member, but more so to a trained counselor who is well versed with similar circumstances. Even when you've not acknowledged your pain, a therapist will help you link your actions to various incidences from your past. Getting professional help also ensures follow up.

The counselor will assess your situation and come up with an approximate duration for your therapy. As the session progresses, you'll continue to open up bit by bit. You may be given some tasks too—such as to call a certain person and apologize, or to write down a list of things that you'd have wanted to tell your loved one before they passed away.

These things are difficult to express at the beginning, but with time it gets easier and the burden gets lighter.

Write It Down

If speaking seems too daunting to begin with, try writing it down. With writing, you're alone with your thoughts, without the feeling of somebody trying to interrogate you. Write exactly how you feel, with as many words as you deem fit. Forget correct grammar or punctuation, just pour your heart out into words.

You may feel broken in the process, as old wounds split open and release secrets they've held on for so long, but all that is part of the process. Look at writing as transferring your burden to that notepad. You can even choose to allow your therapist to go through your journal to get a feeling of those things that you might not be able to express verbally.

Forgive

One of the most crucial components of healing past pain is forgiving those who hurt you. It is definitely not easy. Think of that partner that broke off a relationship that you had invested so much in, that spouse that asked for a divorce after so many years together, that drunk driver who took away your loved one, that family member who raped you as a child, that boss who fired you after all the work that you had put in that job. How can you forgive them after all the anguish they've caused you?

Keep in mind here that forgiveness is for you first. To release you from that mental slavery. Holding onto pain hurts you, not them. It has been said that holding onto a grudge is like taking poison and expecting the other person to die. Unfortunately, if someone is 'dying' here, it's all you. Forgiving them is not doing them a favor—the favor is all yours.

Forgive yourself as well. For the things you did mindlessly in the past that have brought pain to you and others. For that abortion. For that partner that you should have treated better. For the accident, you caused through drunk driving. For going against your parent's advice. Ask for forgiveness where applicable. We all make mistakes, but we can move past that and forge a better future.

Adapt to a New Life

If the trauma has changed your life fundamentally in one way or the other, then start getting accustomed to the new life. If an accident has left you immobile, then start learning how to use a wheelchair. If you've lost a spouse, start getting used to making decisions alone as a widow or widower. Have you lost your business? Consider being employed for some time to get you back on your feet. It's ok to mourn what's lost—but not for too long. Make an effort to get back to the business of living.

Chapter 10: Practice the Mindfulness Approach

Mindfulness involves the conscious focusing of attention on the current moment. It may sound like an easy thing and one that you do all the time—but it's actually not.

Think about it. What are you doing at the moment? You'll find out that you're vacuuming the carpet, while keeping an eye on the baby, and thinking of the doctor's appointment coming up. Oh, you're also listening to that commercial on TV, and it reminds you of your college days. See? Your mind is on multiple things at once. One moment you're in the present, the next you're thinking of the future, then at an instance, you're having a flashback.

When you sit at your desk at work, you're thinking of the report you're working on, and wondering how that finance meeting will go. You're remembering with apprehension the last meeting, and the tense moments as the team tried to explain the dropping profit margins. You've also got an eye on the clock—it's almost lunchtime and the hunger pangs are setting in. you promise yourself to check out that restaurant a block away.

Are these scenarios familiar? We hardly ever think about it, but at any one time, our thoughts are scattered in so many different directions. If you can count them one by one, you'll find about 5 things on your mind at a time. We're constantly overworking our minds. Is it any wonder then that we're so often plagued by stress and anxiety?

Techniques to Practice Mindfulness

The mindfulness approach encourages you to slow down and appreciate the present moment. There are a number of techniques that you can use to practice mindfulness:

Meditation: Sit quietly in a calm place with no distractions. Most people prefer to sit with their legs crossed and arms stretched out, like the basic yoga pose. However, you can sit in any position that you find comfortable. Focus on your breathing. You can add an encouraging or affirming mantra to the meditation. Repeat words such as 'I am healthy and whole' over and over again. Let the thoughts come and go without giving them much attention.

Listen to Your Senses: Look. Listen. Smell. Touch. Taste. Let all your senses be alert to the stimuli around them. Do not overthink the stimuli. Just notice them and let them go.

Body Sensations: Pay attention to the parts of your body in turns. Listen out for tightness, tingling or itching in every part of your body. Start from one point, such as the feet, and proceed all the way up to the head. Focus your mind on that particular sensation and allow your mind to feel it fully.

Emotions: How are you feeling? Are you happy, angry, frustrated, anxious, disappointed or stressed? Accept the emotions without dwelling on them. Just let them be.

Incorporate the Mindfulness Approach to your Daily Life

You do not have to wait until the end of the day to sit in a corner and practice a mindfulness technique. You can practice it in your daily life wherever you are. Let us look at some instances of living in the moment.

- When driving, concentrate on what is happening at that particular moment. Resist the temptation to dwell on the traffic jam, the annoying drivers, that meeting you're getting late for or the alternative routes that you could have taken. Such thoughts will only burden your mind and will not improve the situation in every way. Instead, look at the trees lining the sides of the streets, the walkways, and the people streaming by. Don't analyze them. Just glance at them and allow whichever thoughts to come and go. Listen to hooting cars. Smell the food from the fast-food restaurant nearby. Feel the texture of the steering wheel against your hands. And the pressure of the gas pedals against your foot. As most of the people are stressing themselves silly in the jam, you'll be calm and at peace.

- As you sit in the office, take a few minutes to notice the sensations in your body. Notice those tightening muscles that you've got after sitting for hours. This would be an ideal moment to practice the progressive muscle relaxation technique. Deal with one muscle group at a time. You can start with the feet and gradually travel upwards. Tighten the foot, hold for a few seconds, then release. Repeat as necessary. You should instantly feel the difference between that foot and the other—it will be lighter and more relaxed. The muscle tension should be gone by the time you finish the exercise, and your body will be at ease.

- When you visit the park, sit, inhale and take in the fresh air from nature. Take in deep breaths, letting the air rest in your chest for a bit before exhaling. Notice the birds, the trees, the sky. This is not the time to think about that boss that you can't seem to please, or the bills that are piling up, or the relationship that went south after you had invested so much in it. That, the worrying over all sorts of things when seated on a picnic blanket on the park, would be a terrible waste of an opportunity to live in a beautiful present.

- When you're at the dinner table having your lunch, don't antagonize your mind with the thoughts of all the chores you can't seem to get done. Focus on your food. Inhale the lovely aroma. Notice the ingredients and spices with all the colors and textures that they have. Take a bite, chewing slowly, allowing the flavors to fuse and tantalize your tongue. Notice how the taste of the food changes as you continue to chew. Feel the food go down your throat and imagine all the good that it's doing for your body. Repeat, bite after bite, until you feel the fullness. You will be surprised that half an hour or so has passed with your mind focused on the food, with all the other worries a distance away. By the time you snap back from that positive daze, your mind will be clear and you can then proceed to your other activities with precision.

- During physical exercise, feel the sensations as your body moves. Notice the muscles tense and relax. Feel the pressure on your feet as they land on the jogging track. Notice your emotions shift to more positive ones as the body releases endorphins which make you happier. Feel the waves ride against your skin when swimming. Listen to every sensation, without overemphasizing on them. Let the accompanying thoughts come and go without judgment. If you're exercising outdoors, focus your attention on the elements of nature. Feel the wind in your hair, and the warmth of the sun on your skin.

In addition to the many benefits of physical exercise, practicing mindfulness in the process leaves you with unmatched tranquility.

Starting Out

It is possible that you're so accustomed to multi-tasking in your mind that the idea of focusing on just the present moment sounds untenable. If you're just starting out, you begin by learning how to concentrate. The meditation method works best for beginners. Here you focus on breathing naturally and repeating a phrase.

It may not feel relaxing at first. In fact, in the beginning, you may struggle with the entire concept. The mind takes about 20 minutes or so before it settles, and longer for others. Don't dwell on the difficulty. Go with the flow. Breathe, repeat the phrase, then let those thoughts float away.

If you still can't seem to get the hang of it, find company. Having someone beside you attempting the same technique will encourage you to keep trying. You can also engage a professional, who will observe your practice and recommend improvements that you can take.

Benefits of the Mindfulness Approach

By teaching you how to concentrate on one thing at a time, this approach enhances your focus. Every time you find your thoughts racing, you can now redirect them to concentrate on a particular thing.

One notion that has been repeated severally in the techniques is that of letting the thoughts pass. Here you look at the thoughts as if they're a separate entity from yourself. They come in, and they go. You can apply this technique to other areas of your life. When thoughts of a certain issue are troubling you, you can let them pass. Do not let them turn your mind into a battlefield.

Does this mean that you ignore the issues that you're going through? Absolutely not. We have mentioned before about scheduling a 'worry time', where you think rationally about your problems and take steps towards solving them. Overthinking and worrying does not make any difference. Hence, outside of the worry time, do not dwell on the thoughts—just let them come and go.

By allowing emotions to pass, such as emphasized in one of the mindfulness techniques, you learn about acceptance. You understand that there will be situations that will make you sad, angry or frustrated. It is the nature of life. When the emotions come, you can let them go without judgment.

You don't have to dwell on the one who wronged you. You don't have to question what makes them behave in the manner that they did. You will also not spend time wondering why such a thing would happen to you. You'll simply let it pass.

Mindfulness is an effective technique is dealing with stress, anxiety and panic attacks. These conditions are brought about by constant worrying about what is happening and what may happen in the future. You could suffer from these conditions when dealing with loss, divorce, custody battles, financial constraints, work problem, unstable relationships, and so on.

Whenever you find yourself overwhelmed by the worries, you can let those thoughts pass and shift your attention to your immediate surrounding.

As CBT teaches, your thoughts translate to your actions. If you're restless in mind, it will also manifest physically. You'll be fidgeting and pacing around, attempting to carry out one task of the other, yet not managing to get anything meaningful done. Once you bring some quiet to your mind and allow it to concentrate on something, you will likewise be able to focus on something physically. This allows you to utilize your time properly and get significant work done.

When dealing with a panic attack, 'focusing on the moment' sounds like it will only make everything worse. Here, you can utilize the meditation technique that mostly involves breathing and chanting. Even breathing alone can go if you're too breathless to voice the words. Hyperventilation, which is often caused by panic attacks, causes you to take quick, shallow breaths. This limits the amount of oxygen flowing through your system, further aggravating the situation. Deep breathing introduced an inflow of oxygen aids in getting past the attack.

The mindfulness techniques are simple and can be carried out almost anywhere. When the anxiety seems to be having the better of you, you can take half an hour or so to practice mindfulness and bring your senses back to equilibrium.

Mindfulness works for the situation at hand and also for the future. Like any other skill, it takes practice to perfect. The more you engage in mindfulness, the better you get at it. In the beginning, it takes a lot to clear the mushrooming thoughts from your mind—and even when you do and attempt to focus on the present, one or two stray thoughts will try to intrude. With time, you get better. You're able to focus on the current moment for up to half an hour without any interruptions. Eventually, you'll be a pro, with the ability to snap out of your worries in split seconds and let yourself soak at the moment. Mindfulness is a welcome gift to those suffering from stress and anxiety as well as to those who wish to keep it at bay. Practice it as often as you can, and it'll come in handy in your hour of need.

Conclusion

We're glad that you made it to the end of this book on stress and anxiety management. You may have tried some other remedies before, but now that you're here, we can assume that they did not work. Is CBT the solution for you? Well, we'll leave that decision to you. Our goal here was to ensure that we provide the most comprehensive information on CBT and answer most, if not all of the questions that you may have. We definitely hope that we achieved that to your satisfaction.

Now that you're well informed, you can begin to take action that will free your mind from the negative emotion that has been plaguing you. Have you identified the beliefs and thought patterns that have been fueling your stress, panic attacks, or anxiety? Remember that it is not about the circumstances—but how you respond to them in your mind—that makes the difference.

Formulate a plan to make the changes that you need. Begin to talk to yourself positively. Instead of dwelling on the negative things that you have experienced, cultivate a heart of gratitude by counting what you do have.

Get a partner to walk with you—one that you can speak to comfortably and express the emotions that you're going through. Whether you pick a friend/family member or go to a professional therapist session, the choice is yours, depending on your circumstances. Either way, having some company besides you enhance the chances of adhering to the program and getting rid of your emotional distress for good.

You do not have to effect a radical shift at once. Changing beliefs and thought patterns that have been part of your life for so long is bound to take time. Start writing a healing journal so that you can always note down how you feel and identify the patterns—positive or negative—that form along the way. You will use this information to determine with particular techniques work for you and which ones do not.

Do not give up if you do not see any significant changes right away. Cognitive Behavioral Therapy is no quick fix. The change is slow but sure. You may still experience periods of stress and anxiety along the way, but they should reduce as you go along.

Stress, anxiety, and panic attacks can deal with a big dent in your life. They not only deprive you of the peace and energy you need to attend to your daily activities but also increase your risk of other diseases. Ill health only increases your stress, then it's a downward spiral from there.

This does not have to be your story. You can take charge of your thoughts and steer them towards positivity. You can reset your body and mind to be more aware of the triggers and respond to them appropriately. Managing anxiety or stress is not out of reach—you can utilize this form of therapy to regain your peace and calm and proceed to live your life to the fullest.

Alcohol Addiction: How to Stop Drinking and Recover from Alcohol Addiction

Introduction

Alcoholism is an extreme dependency on consuming alcohol in order to be able to function in society. It also refers to the illnesses of the mind and the extreme behavioral compulsions that are a direct effect of drinking to excess. Alcoholism is a continuous excessive disease that is identifiable by compulsively drinking alcoholic beverages to excess. This practice leads to physical and psychological addiction or dependence. People who are alcoholics are unable to control their drinking. They have no real control over the need to drink often and excessively. This tendency often displays as an inability to go to work regularly or to perform properly when at work. Alcoholics will either socialize way too much or will be unable to socialize with others. Many alcoholics prefer to drink alone, not only because it is quieter and they can focus on the drink but also so there are no other people to judge how much they drink.

Alcoholics are often characterized by their slovenly appearance. When alcoholism takes over most people eventually stop bathing regularly and no longer care about their personal appearance. They do not cut or wash their hair. They do not change clothes regularly, and their clothing is often food-stained and reeking of human body odor. Some alcoholics display violent tendencies. The most mild-mannered person in the world can become a vicious beast or a raving lunatic when the alcohol takes over their senses.

People who are alcoholics are susceptible to certain diseases that do not regularly affect the general public. Alcoholics have an increased risk of developing hepatitis, an inflammation of the tissue in the liver. They are also most likely to suffer from cirrhosis of the liver, which is scarring of the tissue due to the effects of other illnesses that affect the liver. Alcoholics also have an increased risk of developing alcohol poisoning due to the fact that alcoholic beverages are consumed rapidly in a short amount of time.

Alcoholism knows no boundaries. Anyone, anywhere, at any time, can become an alcoholic. It knows no age limit, nor does it prefer one gender over another. Alcoholism does not care if you are rich or you are poor. Alcoholism has been a public health crisis for many generations. This is an amazing fact considering that only about half the people in the world consume all of the alcohol. There are many countries in the world where almost no one drinks any form of alcohol due to religious reasons.

Part of the problem, and part of the reason that alcoholism can so easily become a problem is that alcohol is everywhere. In most towns and cities it is impossible to drive down the street without passing a liquor store, a bar, or a club. Many large cities even advertise their more popular bars. Alcohol can be found at many activities, and many activities grew up around the consumption of alcohol. Consider the college campus and happy hour at the bar. Think of the Friday night mixers and the BYOB (Bring Your Own Bottle) reminder where the host or hostess supplied various mixers. And there are always the holiday gatherings, where even multi-generational families will toast the New Year with a glass of champagne.

So alcoholism does not care where people come from, what they believe, or what they do for a living. Alcoholism is a disease that strikes where it feels like striking and when it feels like striking. Sometimes whole families are alcoholics, and sometimes it is one person in a family of teetotalers. Sometimes one or both parents are alcoholics, but the children never touch a drop. Sometimes the parents do not drink at all, or only socially, and the children become alcoholics. Alcoholics are college graduates and high school dropouts. Alcoholics have jobs and children. Alcoholics drive on the same roads as everyone else.

Numerous negative effects are caused by alcoholism that wreak havoc on the human body. No area of the body is immune to the negative effects of too much drinking. And anyone of these effects has the potential to be life-altering or even deadly.

The communication paths in the brain can be seriously affected by drinking too much. The pathways in the brain control the travel of conscious thought and are created by constantly thinking a thought or practicing a habit. Alcohol can disrupt these pathways and cause differences in the way the brain thinks and reacts to stimuli. It can also create changes in behavior and overall mood. The ability to clearly think and move with grace and ease may be affected.

Excessive drinking can damage the heart. The first effect of drinking on the body is usually a rise in blood pressure to a level that is considered dangerous. Strokes are a direct cause of high blood pressure. Excessive drinking is also responsible for cardiac arrhythmias, where the heart does not beat at a regular pace but suffers irregular beats. This can cause a heart attack. Perhaps the worst effect on the heart is a disease called cardiomyopathy, which is characterized by malformation of the heart muscle that includes drooping or stretching. This physical irregularity can lead to complete heart failure.

The liver is another organ that is directly affected by too much drinking. Once the liver becomes inflamed from too much drinking, the person is at a greater risk of developing hepatitis that may not be curable because of the inflammation of the liver. Excessive drinking can also lead to a condition called fatty liver, where excess fat becomes stored in the liver, and the liver finds it difficult to remove this excess fat because it has suffered damage. Possibly the worst damage to the liver is a disease called cirrhosis which is abnormal scarring of the liver that cannot be replaced by normal liver regeneration. When cirrhosis is involved the only cure is a transplant of a healthy liver.

Most people forget that the effects of alcoholism can also damage the pancreas. The pancreas is the organ that secretes digestive juices into the small intestine to aid in digestion. The pancreas is also responsible for the production and secretion of insulin into the bloodstream. Insulin is the chemical in the body that controls blood sugar.

Besides the enormous health problems that are associated with alcoholism, there are also problems associated with behavior that can harm the drinking person. People who are inebriated often have no fear and might find themselves in dangerous situations. They may try to fight other people. They may engage in harmful activities such as climbing high structures or walking where it might be dangerous. Driving is the worst thing a drunk person can do because they risk not only their own lives but the lives of others.

Alcoholism is a dangerous condition that can have many negative effects on the human body, and consequently, on life itself.

Chapter 1: Alcohol Addiction and Health Challenges

Alcoholism, also known as alcohol addiction, affects people in any area of life. Many experts have studied alcoholics looking for a common factor of what might lead to alcoholism. But alcohol addiction does not care if a person is a male or female, rich or poor, or what color they are or what religion they follow. Unfortunately, no one factor predisposes someone to become an alcoholic. It has no main cause. Behavioral, genetic, and psychological factors all have a contribution to someone developing alcohol addiction.

Alcoholism is a disease. Some people may argue that it is simply a lack of will power, that alcoholics are weak-willed and could quit on their own if they tried hard enough. But this is not the case with alcohol addiction. The excess drinking that causes alcoholism leads to negative changes in the chemistry of the brain. A person who has alcohol addiction may truly be unable to control their own actions.

Alcoholism shows up in various ways. The disease differs in severity between people, how often they drink, and how much they drink. Some people only drink after work is done for the day. Some people drink for several days and then stay sober for a short period. Some people drink heavily throughout the entire day.

The key to alcohol addiction is not the pattern of drinking. The key is that the person is unable to stay sober for more than a short period of time and the person must eventually rely on alcohol to be able to function with some normalcy.

The symptoms of alcohol addiction can be difficult to pinpoint in the individual. Since alcohol is readily available and such a part of many celebrations it is widely considered a socially acceptable beverage. Therefore it may be difficult to know, at least in the beginning, that someone has a problem with alcohol consumption. Society has become adept at turning a blind eye to someone who might have a drinking problem.

Many signs might point to alcohol addiction. Obviously, people with a drinking problem drink much more and much more often than people who do not have a drinking problem. This will give them a higher tolerance than most people, meaning they will need to drink more to feel the effects of the alcohol. Alcoholics often do not have hangovers, perhaps because they are never truly sober. Alcoholics will usually drink at times that other people consider inappropriate. Alcoholics may feel the need to drink as soon as they get out of bed, or they may drink over lunch at work. People with an alcohol addiction do not want to go where there will not be alcohol offered. Those who have an alcohol addiction may leave old friends behind in favor of new, heavy drinking buddies. They will begin to avoid loved ones, and may even lie to them about how much they really drink. They will hide their alcohol, so they always have a secret stash available. Alcoholics have even been known to hide while drinking, such as spending more time than might be necessary in the bathroom or the laundry room. As the disease progresses, the alcoholic will become increasingly dependent on alcohol just to be able to make it through the day. They will begin to experience emotional issues such as depression or extreme anger and will suffer from excessive lethargy. Alcoholics often experience legal problems that come with being arrested for public drunkenness or driving while intoxicated. They may also face demotions at work or even job loss.

Consumption of excessive amounts of alcohol creates effects on the brain that may explain why some people become alcoholics. When people drink the chemical balance in the brain is altered. Alcohol is a downer, a depressant, and it is an attractive legal drug to people who suffer from extreme stress, depression, or a lowered sense of self-worth. After just one drink a person can become much less anxious and much more self-confident. The alcohol lowers the chemical makeup in the part of the brain that has to do with inhibiting feelings. People build a deep desire to drink more alcohol in order to increase positive feelings and reduce the negative ones. This deep desire becomes a craving that can eventually lead to alcoholism.

Unfortunately, genetics may play an important role in deciding who becomes an alcoholic and who does not. Children who grow up with alcoholics are much more likely to become alcoholics themselves. This may also be due to other factors in the environment the child is raised in, but it is believed that genetics has a part in alcohol addiction.
When people speak of environmental factors that may contribute to alcoholism, there are several. Alcohol is available almost anywhere, even in the grocery store or the gas station. People are more likely to drink if people around them are drinking. Alcohol advertisement is everywhere because drinking is supposed to be cool. Drinking is said to elevate a person's status socially. Happy people go to parties and drink a lot.

Alcoholics can suffer from a number of alcohol-related health problems that may or may not be treatable. Frequently consuming too much alcohol can have a negative effect on nearly every system in the body. When someone consumes more alcohol than the body is able to metabolize, the excess is funneled to the bloodstream. The heart will then continuously circulate the alcohol through the body in an effort to locate a place to store it. This leads to changes in the chemistry of the body and affects normal functions of the body.

The body metabolizes most of the alcohol it consumes in the liver. This is why the liver typically suffers so much damage as a result of alcoholism. In the liver, alcohol is changed into a toxic chemical that is known to cause cancer. Excessive drinking causes excess fat to build up in the body, causing a decrease in normal function in the liver. The liver can easily become inflamed, making the body more likely to develop hepatitis. And the increased strain on the liver causes a condition known as cirrhosis, which is scarring in the liver caused by all the other bad effects of alcohol consumption on the liver.

The pancreas, which is the organ responsible for supplying insulin to the body, can also be damaged by excessive and long-term effects of alcohol consumption. The pancreas can become inflamed, and a long period of inflammation can lead to pancreatic cancer.

Chronic excessive consumption of excessive amounts of alcohol can cause an increase in the risk of developing different types of cancer, including cancer of the breast, larynx, stomach, liver, rectum, colon, esophagus, and mouth.

Too much drinking will weaken the function of the immune system. Decreased immunity makes the body vulnerable to many diseases that are caused by infections such as tuberculosis and pneumonia. If these are contracted by a heavy drinker, it will be more difficult for them to recover quickly, if at all, due to their weakened immune systems.

Excessive alcohol consumption causes brain damage. It is the cause of slower reactions, lapses in memory, problems when walking, speech problems such as slurring words or a need to search for words, and vision problems like blurring or double vision. Alcoholics are often injured in falls that happen when they have been drinking because they stumble or are having difficulty seeing obstacles.

People who drink to excess regularly often suffer from poor nourishment and a deficiency in vitamins the body needs to function properly. Alcoholics usually have bad dietary habits. Nutrients from food are not used properly by the body due to reduced function of the gastrointestinal tract. Cells in the body, damaged by the constant onslaught of alcohol, are unable to absorb nutrients properly. The lining of the stomach may break down and begin to bleed, causing poor absorption of nutrients.

Osteoporosis leads to an increased risk of bone breakage and arthritis. Alcohol consumption disrupts the body's ability to absorb vitamin D and calcium, which leads to a drastic weakness in the structure of the bones. Those who drink to excess are more likely to suffer from broken bones than people who do not drink to excess. This is even truer when teens and young adults drink excessively. They can cause changes in the bone structure of the body that will lead to osteoporosis in later years, even if no other risk factors for osteoporosis are present.

Heavy alcohol consumption causes high blood pressure which can lead to strokes. Alcoholics have an increased risk of developing heart failure due to the increased workload the heart suffers trying to filter the excess alcohol out of the body.

Any amount of alcohol consumption can lead to an increase in accidents. Alcoholics often suffer from domestic violence, car wrecks, accidental drownings, slips and falls, and suicide than people who are not alcoholics.

Numerous health benefits will be experienced when a person quits drinking. The first benefit is just a better overall feeling. Without having to constantly process an overabundance of alcohol the body will begin to cleanse itself. The systems in the body regain their natural function and begin to function more closely to normal. The body is no longer required to process so many toxins so it can use that energy for other things. The mind also begins to function better. The mind will be clearer and more focused. Thoughts will be well-focused and will make more sense. The skin will begin to look better, softer and more youthful. Previous skin irritations will begin to clear. Alcohol causes the body to dehydrate, and a lack of hydration causes the skin to dry out and look older. Excessive alcohol consumption also causes the skin on the face to look red because tiny blood vessels break due to high blood pressure. The cells of the body will also function more efficiently. They will be better able to absorb vitamins and nutrients which will make the body healthier overall. Alcohol is a high-calorie drink. People who quit drinking often find they will easily lose weight. And since the alcohol calories are completely devoid of nutrients, replacing them with nutritious foods gives the body access to more natural vitamins. The heart will be healthier. The liver will be cleaner and will enjoy better function.

There are other benefits associated with quitting drinking. Sober people are better able to make connections with other people. Sobriety brings about a renewed desire to connect with friends and relatives, relationships that may have been neglected in favor of a night spent with alcohol. Drinking causes isolation and aloneness. It is more natural to want to connect with other people than it is to connect with alcohol. People who quit drinking will have more time to reconnect with a forgotten hobby or even to learn a new one. Drinking is time-consuming. It takes a lot of time away from more productive activities. Sober people find it easier to sleep better and more regularly. People who quit drinking find it easier to focus and be alert.

Alcoholism is a horribly debilitating disease. It causes massive health problems that can lead to great disability or even early death. It causes numerous mental health problems. Alcoholism not only ruins normal life, but it also takes the place of normal life. Making the decision to quit, and following through, will bring wonderful benefits to the body and the mind, and will enable a return to a more meaningful, fulfilling life.

Chapter 2: How Alcoholism Begins

Alcoholism is a disease marked by the impairment caused by constant and excessive consumption of alcohol. This impairment can directly cause physiological, social, or psychological dysfunction. Alcoholism is not just about how much a person drinks. Many people drink to excess on occasion and are not alcoholics. Alcoholism is more a function of how the alcohol affects the person. If drinking causes other problems in life, then there is a good chance that person is an alcoholic. Unfortunately, alcoholism has become a common disease.

Alcohol addiction often starts quite innocently. People do not start with the idea of being an alcoholic. Alcohol is a drink readily available at many social functions. People gather to drink a few drinks and share good times. The problem starts when people, having seen how good a few drinks made them feel at the party last week, take a drink to relieve the stress of a long work day. Whenever someone begins drinking to relieve stress, or to mask any other problem, they are setting a dangerous precedent. Because once alcohol is used as a problem solver or a problem masker, the stage is set for the beginning of alcoholism.

Being able to understand how alcohol addiction begins and how it develops can make it easier to realize when there is a problem with oneself or a loved one. Knowing how alcoholism works makes it easier to fight against.

In the early stages of alcoholism, people begin to have negative experiences that are directly related to excess drinking. These negative experiences include blackouts, violence toward other people, arguments with those closest to them, and hangovers. A hangover is an aftereffect of too much drinking the night before. It is marked by headache, fatigue, excessive thirst, dry mouth, and nausea. A blackout is just what it says it is: the person drinking has blacked out the memory of the time they were drinking. They have little to no memory of the night before. During the early stage of alcoholism, people notice their tolerance is increasing. They must constantly drink more and more alcohol to get the same good feeling they did before. They may begin to seek out new locations to drink and new people to drink with, so no one will know exactly how much they are really drinking.

In the middle stage of alcoholism, life begins to unravel. The person starts to lose control of their life. They will usually deny that any kind of problem exists. But now the person is drinking more than they were before. In this stage, the addiction is firmly set. People who try to stop drinking without outside help are often not successful. Work life may begin to slide downhill, and personal life offers more problems than solutions. They may begin to treat the morning hangover with an early drink, a little 'hair of the dog.' Also in this stage, the person begins to experience depression or anxiety. And even the presence of problems directly associated with drinking, like legal problems or emotional and physical problems are not enough to make them stop drinking.

Anyone who drinks long enough will eventually reach the last stage of alcoholism. In this stage, the person has totally lost control of everything. They no longer have meaningful personal relationships, because all the important people in their lives have likely left them. They may have lost their job and are probably experiencing severe financial problems. This is also the stage where excess drinking has caused enough health problems that the person's health has begun to seriously fail. At this point, if the person wants to quit drinking, they will definitely require professional assistance. If they do not drink, they will experience symptoms of withdrawal that might include sleep issues, irritability, nausea, profuse sweating, and tremors. The person may experience hallucinations or delusional thinking.

But where does alcoholism come from? The answers to that are extremely varied. While alcohol addiction begins with the act of drinking, many different factors will cause a person to tend towards becoming an alcoholic.

Sometimes drinking to excess is a family habit. There are those families that always have alcohol at every family function. Any excuse is a good excuse to have a drink. These families often have an addiction to other things too. They may overeat, overdo competition in sports, or constantly strive to be better than every other family on the block. People usually do not have just one addiction; people usually have addictive personalities and alcohol is the drug of choice.

Stress can cause people to drink excessively. Often people will take a drink in order to relieve the stresses of the day. In the early stages of alcohol addiction, people discover that a few social drinks will wash away the cares of the day. A little alcohol makes everything look and feel better. They remember this feeling and, when they have had a bad day, they take a drink or two just to 'take the edge off things.' Soon they are taking a few drinks whenever they have a bad day. Then a few drinks lead to a few more drinks.

Drinking to ease stress levels and drinking to self-medicate go hand in hand. Taking a few drinks to relieve the daily stress is one way to self-medicate. Sometimes people drink to hide the pain from a physical injury. More commonly people drink to hide the pain from an emotional hurt. People drink to dull the pain they feel when a loved one dies. People drink to erase the pain of a love that has gone wrong. People drink to hide feelings of inadequacy in social situation. Sometimes people drink to hide the pain from some sort of abuse or neglect.

And some people will drink to cover up the failures they feel in life. People who were turned down for a promotion, people who otherwise hate their professional life, those who cannot stand their family life— these are all people who drink to cover up the failures of life they have experienced. Their lives have not turned out as they hoped, so they drink to feel better about themselves.

Alcoholism begins quietly and attacks without warning. It can begin innocently, with one or two drinks, until the day it turns into an evil monster that takes over life.

Chapter 3: The Enabler

Most alcoholics would not remain alcoholics very long without the assistance of an enabler. The enabler helps the alcoholic hide their addiction from the world. The enabler is the person who faces all the bad things about alcoholism so the alcoholic can continue to pretend that there is nothing wrong with their drinking, that no real problem exists in their world.

The enabler is not willing to admit that there is a problem with the alcoholic. They will either overlook the existence of the problem or pretend that the problem does not exist, that it is all in someone else's mind.

To the enabler, the addict is never the person at fault. The problem lies with everyone else. Either the boss was too hard, the job was too demanding, the kids are too noisy, traffic was bad—the problem is never the fault of the addict and always the fault of anything or anyone else.

Fear is often a great motivator for the enabler. Often addicts act irrationally or angrily. They may blame all of life's problems on the enabler. Their behavior is often so frightening that the enabler will go to any length possible to avoid situations where the alcoholic will have reason to find fault with them.

The enabler will lie about anything and everything. The enabler will lie to the alcoholic's boss and claim they are sick yet again. The enabler will pretend extenuating circumstances are preventing them from coming to yet another family function or gathering of friends. They will always put the blame on themselves.

The addict will always come first in the eyes of the enabler. In the life of the enabler, the addict's needs will always be more important, even if it means neglecting their own needs. While wanting to help loved ones is normal, the enabler takes it much farther than that.

Enablers often experience great difficulty in showing emotions. They often have problems showing their innermost feelings, especially if they think the addict will subject them to negative thoughts, words, or actions for doing so.

The enabler takes care of many basic functions for the alcoholic, so they avoid much of the negative aspects of being an addict. The enabler will always make sure that there is enough of the right kind of alcohol in the house. The enabler will clean up any messes that the enabler makes, whether it is breaking a lamp in a drunken stagger through the house or even vomiting while intoxicated. The enabler will lie to others and make excuses for the alcoholic, even going so far as to take all the blame for the situation themselves. And the enabler will endure abject abuse from the alcoholic so that no one else will need to suffer their abuse. The enabler goes out of their way to make the situation seem better than it really is so that the alcoholic feels free to continue their downward spiral.

Chapter 4: Choosing to Quit Drinking and Its Benefits

Alcohol is everywhere. Just like food, it is an item often found at family gatherings, social events, and just about any kind of celebration imaginable. Many people use alcohol to cope with life's events. People drink to celebrate the arrival of new babies and the passing of loved ones. Alcohol is used to celebrate achievements and mourn over failures. And do not forget happy hour and the weekend.

Since alcohol and its use are so prevalent in today's society, making the decision to quit is not always easy. It can be a struggle for anyone, even the person with the greatest personal determination. When an alcoholic decides to quit drinking it is not a temporary decision, like a new diet or training for a marathon. When an alcoholic stops drinking it must be a lifelong decision. What makes a person an alcoholic is the inability to control their own drinking, to regulate the amount of alcohol consumed and how often it is consumed. For an alcoholic to be successful when quitting drinking they must never take another alcoholic drink ever again, not even one drop. This in itself can be a daunting task.

Changing any habit requires hard work, and drinking is a habit. Many people do not succeed the first time they decide to quit drinking, because drinking is not just a bad habit. Alcohol causes physical changes in the body that must also be addressed if quitting is to be successful. Failure is common, but it is not the end. Learn from failure and try again. Every try will be another step toward the goal. And if one method of quitting does not work, then try another method.

For someone to quit drinking alcohol requires a personal decision. No one can decide that another person should quit drinking. Even if the alcoholic is an underage person, they will not quit drinking just because they are told to. Love will not make someone else quit drinking. Neither will threats, tears, promises or even leaving them to their own devices. The alcoholic must make the decision because the path to sobriety is mainly a solo trip.

The alcoholic will not completely quit drinking until they are able to accept that they have a problem and want to change. The alcoholic does not care about lost jobs or lost family. They will simply drown their sorrows in another drink. They do not care if their friends abandon them because their one true friend, the bottle, is still there. The bottle never tells them they are a failure. The bottle never tells them the relationship is over or that they are no longer welcome here. The bottle loves them.

An alcoholic will not truly be ready to quit until they hit bottom, whatever their personal bottom is. The ultimate depth of failure is different for every person, and every person must hit that depth so they can go no lower. They must give up all their twisted notions of doing things their own way and be ready to accept outside help to curb this addiction. Because while the path to sobriety is a mostly personal path, it will require assistance from outside forces. And the alcoholic must be ready to accept this help in order to be successful. And they are the only ones who can make that decision.

If the decision to quit has been made that is the first step toward success. Tell everyone. Do not worry about what might happen if this goal is not successful. It might not be, but that is no reason not to try. Tell friends and family members that quitting drinking is the plan. Explain why the decision was made. People need to know and understand why personal habits have suddenly changed, why trips to the local bar or invitations out are suddenly being declined. Then people will be able to stop issuing those tempting invitations. And any little successes can be shared with everyone.

It will be best in the beginning to avoid all the places where drinking has historically occurred. This will also be a personal decision for the alcoholic to make. Favorite drinking spots are different for each person. It might be the local bar. It might be a favorite local restaurant. It will be necessary to avoid trivia night or the bowling league if those are occasions to drink. Any place that has ever been a place to go to consume alcohol must now be studiously avoided in order to remove possible temptation. In the beginning, the will power is too weak to simply think it is okay to go to familiar places and not drink.

Search past habits to see the particular times when drinking was more likely to be a focus. Is happy hour a problem? Is a liquid lunch a habit? Is it a regular practice to head to the bar on Friday or Saturday night after work? Write down all the times when having a drink would be a normal practice. This is especially important in order to be able to avoid these times. Drinking at a particular time is another habit that must be broken.

And definitely clear out all the little stashes of alcohol. Clean out the house. Search everywhere there might be some alcohol stashed. Ask others to help search if needed. It will be important to get all traces of alcohol out of the house before quitting.

Again, drinking is a habit that causes physical changes. Because of the physical changes, it causes it may be more difficult to stop drinking than to end other bad habits. Alcohol is a substance that causes addiction by activating the receptors in the brain that give pleasure. Every time these pathways are activated and give off pleasure signals, it gets harder and harder to get pleasure signals from these pathways. That is why alcohol is such a tough addiction to break because it has built to such a strong level over time.

So to quit drinking it will be necessary to not only make a mental decision but also to help the body support that decision physically. The body will need to be as strong as possible to fight this fight. After long term drinking, the body is probably malnourished and greatly in need of important nutrients. Start with frequent small meals of healthy nourishing foods. Proteins, fruits, and vegetables will become new best friends. Try to stay away from snack foods. These foods will not give the level of nutrition that the body needs right now, and the brain may associate them with drinking and start sending out cravings.

It might be helpful, before quitting, to make an effort to remove as much stress from everyday life as possible. Life itself is stressful and quitting drinking is even more stressful. If any of this stress can be removed, it will greatly increase chances of success. Set up direct deposit and automatic bill pay if possible. That will leave one less thing to worry about and will guarantee the bills get paid on time. Make weekly menus and prepare as much food as possible in advance. Clear space in the closet to line up a week's worth of clothing choices so it will only be necessary to grab that day's outfit and get dressed. Chose a gym buddy and set up a workout schedule. Any changes that can be made early will serve to remove much of the everyday decision making and allow focus to be spent on not drinking.

Be prepared to accept the physical symptoms that go along with quitting drinking. These are many and may include depression, excessive perspiration, sleep problems, shakiness, uneasiness, mood swings, and an increase in feelings of anxiety. These are what is known as withdrawal symptoms and can last anywhere from a few days to a few weeks. It just depends on how long the person has been drinking to excess.

And remember that this is a lifelong fight. This journey has no end. That is why people who quit drinking are called recovering alcoholic. Alcohol addiction is something that is always being recovered from. It will never be over. There is no cure.

But there are many benefits to quitting drinking. These include physical, mental, and emotional benefits as well a lifestyle and monetary changes.

Besides the obvious health changes—the clearer skin and eyes, stopping damage to the heart and liver—there are other health changes that are not often associated with drinking. Besides causing facial flushing excessive drinking can cause skin irritations like acne and eczema. The headaches that regularly follow a night of drinking will be a thing of the past. The dark circles under the eyes will gradually disappear. Sleep will come easier and will be deeper and more meaningful. Excessive consumption of alcohol causes malfunctions in a person's sex life, so quitting drinking will definitely lead to an improvement.

The excessive use of alcohol will cause an increase in anxiety and depression, even though people often turn to alcohol to deal with feelings of anxiety and depression. Once a person quits drinking these feelings will gradually return to a level where they can be more easily managed. Mood swings will gradually decrease. People who have quit drinking find they have better control over their everyday emotions. Granted they will need to learn other ways of coping with emotions besides drinking, but this will help lead to an overall better sense of self-worth.

People who quit drinking eventually find their mind is clearer and thoughts come easier. They forget things less than they did when they were drinking. They are better able to focus on the important things in life. Sober people are able to focus on the reason behind things and not look at everything emotionally.

Besides alcohol dependency, there are other major health effects to be concerned with. Even if excessive drinking does not currently affect health, it can lead to diseases that do not appear until years later. Some of the damage done to major organs may not be able to be healed or reversed. Structural changes in the brain may be improved. Quitting drinking can also assist with reversing the effects of alcohol on attention span, memory, and thinking ability, all of which alcohol affects negatively.

The decision to quit drinking must be a purely personal decision for purely personal reasons. No one became an alcoholic overnight, and no one can hope to be better overnight. It will take hard work and discipline. It will almost certainly be necessary to ask for outside help; in fact, sometimes the more help one has, the better their recovery will be. The road will not be easy, and failure will most certainly happen. But the rewards are too great to ignore.

Chapter 5: Best Method to Stop Drinking

Anyone who seriously thinks they might have a serious drinking problem probably does. So instead of asking that question, ask if drinking is causing a problem with the enjoyment of everyday life. Ask exactly what effect alcohol is having on maintaining relationships. These questions will give insights to the problems currently being faced. No one should ever compare their own level and style of alcohol consumption to anyone else. Every addiction is personal just like every journey to sobriety will be personal.

Once the decision has been made to stop drinking it is important to list all the reasons that exist to stop drinking and accept them. No problem can be properly addressed unless it is accepted for what it is. Accept that an alcohol addiction exists and must be conquered in order to live a longer, more fulfilling life.

So how does one quit drinking? Well, the obvious answer is to stop buying alcoholic beverages and never drink another drop of anything alcoholic. That is basically what happens when someone quits drinking.

But many different methods can be successfully used to help someone beat the pains of alcoholism.

One method that many people try, and many more think of trying, is a gradual decrease in the amount of alcohol that is consumed. Using this method will greatly decrease the possibility of suffering from alcohol-related withdrawal symptoms. Some of the symptoms that go along with suddenly quitting drinking are sleep disturbances, excessive sweating, tremors, headaches, anxiety, and depression. The idea behind gradually decreasing consumption is to hopefully lessen or eliminate these symptoms. These symptoms can possibly be quite severe, so attempting to quit drinking or at least to cut down on one's own without medical assistance would make tapering off a better option.

The easiest way to cut down on alcohol consumption is to reduce the actual number of alcoholic drinks consumed daily. This system is easy enough to follow. If the normal number of drinks taken daily is ten, then cut that down to eight for a while. How long it will take to feel more normal at the reduced level depends mostly on how many withdrawal symptoms are experienced and to what degree of severity. It may take several days for the withdrawal symptoms to cease. Then cut down the number of drinks again.

Other methods of tapering off include putting a greater amount of time in between individual drinks. If one drink each hour is normal, then drink one drink every two hours. Some people may stick to the one drink per hour schedule, but every other drink is water or a sports drink. Some people will alternate the every-other-hour drink with an alcoholic beverage they do not like the taste of, with the idea they will not drink a drink they do not like.

Tapering off is not a forever process. It needs to have an end date. So before beginning a system of cutting down on alcohol consumption, the most important part is to set an exact schedule the tapering off will follow along with a set date to stop drinking completely. And tapering off will not work for everyone with an alcohol addiction. Cutting down on the amount of alcohol consumed simply does not work for everyone, and it is nowhere near as effective a method for quitting alcohol as it is with other substances. Tapering off simply works better with nicotine or prescription drugs. Those who fail with this method are usually long term drinkers or those who can be considered heavy drinkers. It is also usually not successful for people who lack some sort of outside support system or are surrounded constantly by the triggers that led to alcohol addiction.

Doing a detox at home is not the best method for beating an addiction to alcohol. It may only be successful for those who have not been drinking long enough to form a strong addiction. It is a less expensive option and may work for those people who are not yet struggling with the negative effects of alcohol addiction.

Some medications are approved for treating alcohol addiction. One of these medicines is disulfiram, which is also known as Antabuse. It was the drug first approved by the FDA for use in individuals with alcohol addiction. Antabuse changes the chemistry inside the body to make people become violently ill if they drink an alcoholic beverage. It will work for people who are motivated to take it regularly. The problem is that people may have trouble taking a drug they know will cause the symptoms of a really awful hangover—sweating, vomiting, and headaches. But it does work when taken daily. It might also be appropriate for people who only feel the need to take a medication to counteract times they may be tempted to cheat.

Another medication that might be used for the treatment of alcohol addiction is the drug naltrexone. This drug works by suppressing the good feelings that come with drinking. So people can drink when they take naltrexone, and they will feel drunk, but they will not feel any of the good feelings generally associated with drinking. This medication can also help keep cravings at bay also. Usually when the alcoholic thinks about drinking the brain sends out feelings of pleasure. With naltrexone, these feelings are suppressed. This drug generally works best with someone who has already quit drinking.

Acamprosate, also known as Campral, is effective in relieving the symptoms of withdrawal that come with quitting drinking. Since withdrawal symptoms might last for many months after quitting drinking this drug can be an important part of recovery. The biggest drawback to Campral is the dosage amount. It usually requires taking two pills three or four times daily. This would not work for someone who is bad at remembering to take pills or does not like taking pills regularly.

Since alcohol has been around since the dawn of time, alcohol addiction has also been around that long. Before the last hundred years or so there was only one way known to man to quit drinking, and that was to go 'cold turkey,' to completely quit drinking any form of alcohol immediately, without the benefit of medication or tapering. Cold turkey is still in use today. But quitting drinking cold turkey should never be attempted without the supervision of a medical professional. Many alcoholics who stop drinking will suffer from severe symptoms of withdrawal including grand mal seizures from the convulsions and confusion of a severe level. These people may also suffer from cardiac arrhythmias and fevers that are dangerously high. People who have drunk excessive amounts over a long period are more likely to be affected by the most severe withdrawal symptoms. Also, consider that people who have been addicted to alcohol for a long time are most like undernourished and may not have the energy reserves to fight off the withdrawal symptoms effectively. And severe dehydration may affect people who are withdrawing from alcohol abuse. This can lead to a massive imbalance of electrolytes in the body that could lead to extreme confusion and a malfunction of the nerves and their responses.

Perhaps the most widely used method to quit drinking is the use of rehabilitation and detoxification. This is done during an in-patient setting at a medical facility. This method can be time-consuming and expensive, but it may be the only method that truly works for people with a deeply ingrained addiction. The level of care will depend greatly on the level of addiction.

Entering a treatment center for alcohol addiction is a totally voluntary decision. While entering treatment may be mandatory as part of a court sentence, it is still mainly a voluntary decision. The alcoholic must decide to go to treatment. Rehabilitation (rehab) centers are not like going to jail. There are no locks on the doors. The patient can leave at any time they chose to. There are house rules, and one of these rules is that continued alcohol and/or drug use will not be tolerated.

Some rehab facilities will offer detox services, and others will require that detoxing is done before entering the facility. Detox, or detoxification, refers to the process of cleansing the body of its immediate need for regular consumption of alcohol. Detoxing is the step number one in treating alcohol addiction. This is the time when alcohol is flushed completely out of the body. This is also when the symptoms of withdrawal will begin. As the body intakes less alcohol is will begin to suffer the ill effects of quitting. These symptoms generally stop within the first week or two but may end faster or last much longer depending on the level of addiction. These symptoms often make people fear to quit drinking because of the fear of these symptoms. That is why detox should be done under the care of a medical professional and possibly in a treatment center.

Once the worst symptoms of detox have passed, the alcoholic is ready to enter a treatment facility. These facilities are residential, meaning the person will live there for the duration of the initial treatment period. Treatment will fall into several phases but the first phase, the most intense, will be conducted on an in-patient basis. Rehab facilities vary in design from strict boot-camp style housing to something that more closely resembles a five-star hotel. The difference depends on the amount of money the patient can spend and what type of treatment they personally prefer. Keep in mind that the beauty or lack thereof in the facility has almost nothing to do with how successful they will be in making and keeping someone sober.

All rehab centers share one common trait: a severe lack of personal privacy. The patient will bring their own clothing and toiletries, but upon arrival, their bag will be checked for hidden sources of alcohol. Personal cell phones, laptops, and tablets usually are not allowed. There will be no contact with the outside world for at least two weeks. The idea is to make a complete break with the world the alcoholic could not function in and open up their minds to the possibility of a different way of life.

The basic component of all rehab centers is education. While the process will vary between facilities, it is all about getting people to take a more realistic and honest view of their personal addiction. They will also work to help the patient carefully examine the way they view alcohol use. During the early days of rehab, the vast majority of alcoholics will still hold on to some level of denial about how serious their problem really is. They may also be unsure of the fact that they really do have a problem. They may be denying that there is a problem, insisting they do not belong in rehab.

Classes in rehab will focus on alcoholism and its negative effects. One of the hardest things for alcoholics to accept is that they are suffering from a disease. It is difficult for people to believe that something that began as a socially accepted activity has turned into a disease. And a large part of the problem in treating alcohol addiction is that while individuals with alcohol addiction are held responsible for their actions they are usually not able to withstand the power of the alcohol that makes them act the way they do. So the patient will learn ways to counteract the mental effects of alcohol. They will also spend time learning what consequences they will face if they continue to use alcohol.

Rehabilitation makes use of group therapy and individual counseling. Group therapy will depend heavily on the individual's ability to talk about their problems in public. While the reason they are in rehab is probably similar to the reason everyone else is there, each patient will have a distinctly different back story. Everyone's path to alcohol addiction is different, just as everyone's path to sobriety will be quite different. The purpose of group therapy is twofold: point out dishonesty and assist with those who really want to succeed. Groups in group therapy are usually made up of patients in different levels of recovery and perhaps even some who have already graduated from inpatient therapy. They will be quick to point out when an addict is not completely honest about the nature of their addiction. People who cannot be honest about their addiction cannot possibly hope to recover.

Group members are also quite willing to help those who really want help. And the patients learn to accept help from others who have gone before.

Individual counseling may also be part of the program. Some individuals will benefit greatly from the opportunity to have one-on-one counseling sessions with a personal counselor. The patient may feel some problems are too intense to share in group therapy, or they may have a series of deeply buried problems that need the guiding help a personal therapist can give. The individual counseling sessions may sometimes include family members. This is especially important since the patient will not have a meaningful recovery without the help and guidance of close family members and friends. And most rehab programs will require family members' attendance at counseling sessions apart from those with the patient.

An average day in a rehab facility begins with waking early for a hearty, healthy breakfast in the patient's dining room. Meals are not served in the room like in a hospital. Then there will be meditation groups, counseling groups, yoga, or some physical activity. After returning to the dining room for lunch, there will be more counseling with an emphasis on group sessions or family sessions. Late afternoon might see more physical activity, always some group activity like walking together on a trail or joining in a sport. Then, after a healthy dinner, it is time for shower and sleep. The entire schedule is designed to create a highly structured schedule for the patient, mainly so they can learn how to get structure back into their daily lives and so they can learn to take instructions from others. This will be especially important for the time following in-patient rehab.

The inpatient portion usually lasts four to eight weeks, depending on the facility and the level of treatment the patient requires, although some intensive programs can last up to one year. During the inpatient phase, the patient will learn many things about their addiction. They will also have learned how to take instructions from others regarding their addiction and will have learned how to depend on others for assistance in defeating their addiction. They will have learned to ask for help when they need it. This is especially important for the next phase of care where they will be back out in the world and will need to rely on outpatient plans.

After completing the in-patient part of the rehabilitation process, the patient is ready to leave the facility and begin outpatient therapy. This part of the program is especially critical, and it is where many fail, at least on the first try, because they are back in the real world without specialized guidance. No one is telling them when to eat breakfast or make their bed or go to group meeting. Now is when the alcoholic truly begins to understand living life without the alcohol crutch. Hopefully family and friends are there to lend support, but most of the burden falls on the alcoholic. And this is precisely why rehab is focused so heavily on the patient joining activities and speaking in group whether they wanted to or not. In the outside world, the patient needs to be able to ask for help when they need it.

No matter what method of quitting drinking is used, some form of counseling will be part of the process. This might mean that the patient continues to see a counselor for individual and/or group session. There will be separate family counseling for the family of the alcoholic, and there will be group counseling with the alcoholic and the family involved.

The counselor who assists alcohol addicted persons will know that everyone's recovery process is different. Each patient is a unique individual who will need a treatment plan geared specifically toward that individual. In the first few months following treatment at the rehab center the meeting with the counselor will be frequent, as many as four or five a week if needed. These meetings are important to help the recovering alcoholic stay on the right path. And the counselor, or a trusted colleague, will always be available by phone if a strong urge comes up during an off-meeting time.

The alcohol counselor will take an in-depth history of the patient's personal struggles with alcohol, and it is important the patient leaves nothing out. The more information the counselor has, the better the treatment plan will be. The counselor will set a plan for the patient's individual recovery, a sort of schedule of milestones the counselor hopes to achieve. They will discuss, in great detail, the things that led the patient to seek the comfort of alcohol in the first place. Because, after all, alcohol is a comfort, a coping mechanism, and ways to find the same comfort without drinking must be taught to the alcoholic. The counselor will also provide periodic assessments of progress and may reorganize the treatment plan if needed.

Recovery is not impossible, but it is a lifelong process that will require strict attention and much hard work. But, once abstinence becomes a way of life, the personal rewards are endless.

Chapter 6: Kill the Cravings

Once the alcoholic has embarked on a life of sobriety, there should be no more consumption of alcohol, ever. Remember an alcoholic is always in recovery, and even one drink can send a person back down the spiral into alcoholism. So it is important to abstain from drinking forever.

Unfortunately, the cravings still exist. A craving is a strong mental or physical urge to eat or drink something. A craving pulls a person's thoughts in one direction only, and the focus is this thing that must be consumed. If the alcoholic gives in to these cravings for alcohol, they will be right back where they started.

These cravings, or urges, are usually controllable with a little planning and effort. After time urges will gradually lessen. This is because new pathways of information have been laid out in the brain. Where before the craving would send a message to tell the body to drink, now when the craving hits the body sends back the confusing message that it is going to do something other than drink alcohol. At first, the mind will be quite confused. But with time those old pathways will be shut down and replaced with new pathways and the urges to drink will begin to subside.

There are two types of events that can cause an urge to drink. These are called 'triggers.' The triggers that are external come from everyday life and the things, places, people, and events that make up the external world. The other type of trigger is internal and may be more confusing, and therefore harder to control, to the recovering alcoholic.

Triggers caused by external events can sometimes be relatively easy to control. If the daily happy hour was formerly a time to drink, then happy hour will not be a future destination. If the weekend barbeques overflowed with beer, then the beer needs to be left in the store. The trick is to either reprogram the mind to enjoy certain events alcohol-free or to avoid those events altogether. Sometimes people cause a trigger. The boss is being unreasonable, so a quick nip is in order. This may be the time to decide if the boss is being unreasonable or if the problem is really internal. If friends want to go on a pub crawl, the answer is certainly 'no.' This will likely mean changing old habits and losing old friends, but it is vital to the recovery process.

Triggers that come from within can be harder to figure out because there is no obvious event to place the blame on. The urge to have a drink just seems to appear out of nowhere. These urges will need to be examined in great detail by the recovering alcoholic, perhaps with the help of his counselor, to determine exactly what set off the urge to drink. For example, if before the alcoholic drank to ease the pain of a headache, then a headache caused by too much time in the sun might cause an urge to drink. This is the time for the alcoholic to be completely honest with themselves and overlook nothing, no matter how trivial it might seem.

The counselor will be available for those times when a craving cannot be ignored. And there will be other groups that will assist the alcoholic on the path to recovery.

It might also help to engage in something the person used to love doing or to learn something new. This might be a good time to reconnect with a love of art or keeping a journal. A journal is an especially good idea because the patient can write down anything they think or feel and it is completely private until they chose to share it. Maybe the person used to play volleyball or weekend pickup games of basketball at the neighborhood park. Get back to doing the activities that once brought happiness to life. It might be time to try something new. Recovery is all about breaking out of old habits and forming new ones. Maybe it's time to try ballroom dancing or poetry reading. A new high-risk skill might be in order too. Since alcoholics crave the rush that alcohol brings, maybe that rush could be found elsewhere, perhaps with skiing or boxing.

The possibilities are endless. The important thing is to realize that this is the path to a new more meaningful life and the script has not been written. This phase of life can be anything the recovering alcoholic wants it to be and now is the time to take advantage of that opportunity.

Chapter 7: Change Thoughts and Mindset

Now is the time for a whole new mindset. Remember, this is all about starting life over. The past is gone because it cannot be changed anyway. It is now time to look forward, believing that every day is a new day and recovery is possible.

Beginning this new phase of life requires resetting processes in the mind. Remember, habits are formed when the mind lays down a nerve pathway to a particular spot in response to a constant stimulus. One simple example is learning to flip a pancake in the pan. By putting the flipper under the pancake and turning the wrist, the pancake should flip over to the other side for cooking. But this might not happen in the beginning. The nerve path has not been laid. During practice, the nerve pathway becomes stronger until it is finally set. So when the flipper is slid under the pancake, this is the stimulus that travels to a point in the brain that sends a message telling the wrist to turn is a specific way in order to turn the pancake over in the pan. It sounds complicated, but this is what the mind does daily, and the mind is very good at it.

The activities and behaviors that the patient engages in after rehab are much like this. When a routine is practiced often, the mind develops very deep pathways with a thin layer of insulation surrounding them. This is to allow the signal to travel faster and easier. And just like current habits are easy to perform, new activities and behaviors will eventually become habits.

The mind is a powerful tool on the path to sobriety. The first step to creating new mind paths is to acknowledge the existence of the old ones. Pay particular attention to negative thoughts that will put mental blocks in the path to recovery. Change negative thoughts into positive ones. You do deserve this new life. You are strong enough to achieve this goal. You will remain sober. In the beginning, the mind may try to negate these thoughts. It's sort of like the good angel and the bad angel sitting on one's shoulder. Do not let the bad angel win.

The recovering alcoholic may be forced to find new places to go where alcohol will not be a temptation. Obviously, the bar is now off limits because the temptation will be too great. Even walking in the door and smelling the alcohol in the floating haze will be enough of a trigger to bring back the drinking. But what about other places where alcohol might be served? If the function is at home, then make it alcohol-free. You can do what you want in your own house. Do not serve alcohol, and make it very clear during the invitation process that no alcohol will be allowed on the premises. The home is a personal safe space and should be kept safe. But think about events like concerts and sporting events, where alcohol is served. If the path to the seat can be routed somewhere other than right past the alcohol vendors, that would be a good thing. Maybe the plan is to go to the seat first and let someone else go for refreshments. If there is no viable option, then it may be necessary to avoid these events, at least in the beginning when resistance might still be weak.

Unfortunately the recovering alcoholic will likely be forced to find a new set of friends. The old friends who still go on pub crawls and weekend binges will not understand this new sober lifestyle. Hanging out with them just increases the urges to drink and the possibility that a relapse can occur. So as much as it might hurt in the beginning, it might be better to leave them behind. But turn this into a positive by thinking of the rewards offered by this new lifestyle. Not only is alcohol a thing of the past, opening up a whole new future, but there are so many new people to be discovered. Whether these new friends come from the rehab center, group therapy, church, scheduled meetings, or new hobbies discovered, the possibilities are endless. The chance to make so many new friends will make life feel exciting and new.

Chapter 8: Recovery Plan

One of the most important parts of alcohol recovery is to have a plan in place to facilitate that recovery. No goal is ever reached without a plan. The key is knowing what to do next, so there is little to no room for error when the alcoholic reenters the real world outside of rehab. This plan will contain goals and activities that will give the recovering alcoholic guidance for coping with the outside world.

The recovery plan needs to be set up by the recovering alcoholic because it is their plan. It is personal to them. It will list everything they need to know and to do to get started on the path to recovery and stay on track.

One important part of the plan will include those things that make the alcoholic feel better, those things that lead to a feeling of wellness. These are simple things, events no more complicated than quiet time at home, exercising, family time, walks in the park, reading, or soaking in the bathtub. The list will consist of simple, no-cost activities that can be done without much travel or complexity. These are the things that make the person feel good inside, and these activities will be used to replace the old activities that led to drinking. Review these items at least daily, more often if it helps make the path to sobriety easier to walk. These activities will bring about positive thoughts that will help erase the negative thoughts that led to excessive drinking.

Make a list of known triggers. Make this list as comprehensive as possible. Most alcoholics know those events that will set off the cravings for alcohol. Be brutally honest. If the kids' screaming happily while playing is a trigger, then write that down, it can be addressed and acted upon as needed. The key is to list everything. This is where the alcoholic will discover those things that cause cravings so that a plan can be put into place to either avoid these events or to fix them if they cannot be avoided completely. Going to the local bar can be avoided. Stress at work cannot be avoided.

The alcoholic must know and list their own personal warning signs that the cravings are about to take over the common sense. Only be recognizing these triggers can a person hope to defend against them. Again, write them down and be brutally honest. They cannot be fixed if they are not known. If being isolated from other people causes feeling of cravings then perhaps regular trips to the park, a cultural event, or even church will make the person feel less isolated and more a part of society. If being irritable or angry triggers desires to drink then a new coping mechanism must be determined as it is nearly impossible to go through life and never be angry or irritated. Perhaps the strategy here would include a few minutes of quiet meditation or a brisk walk around the block. Whatever the coping strategies are they must be personal and actionable. And if a particular strategy does not work, then change it.

And since major crises will happen in everyone's life, a plan must be in place to help the recovering alcoholic cope with crises. These fall into two categories: the ones that the individual can handle with someone else's assistance and the ones where the individual has totally lost control.

If the problem is one that the alcoholic can handle with assistance, then there are numerous resources at their disposal. It then is simply a matter of reaching out for help. Certainly, the alcoholic should be able to turn to family members to help them get through an intense craving or major life event. Sometimes greater help is needed. This would be the time when a person would turn to their personal counselor to talk to while trying to cope. They may have kept in touch with other patients from the rehab center. If so then now is the time to call them. They understand better than anyone the struggle the alcoholic is facing and would be well equipped to helping them cope. A buddy from a support group is another option. They are tasked with helping their partner on their travels toward sobriety, just as someone gives them the same type of assistance.

There may be times when the recovering alcoholic is beyond private help and must be referred to a professional. A relapse into drinking is one of these times, certainly, but there are others not related to actual drinking. The person may have become extremely agitated or violent over some happening and may need a visit to the doctor or a medical facility. The important thing is to recognize the possibility of these behaviors before they happen and to decide at what point outside intervention is needed.

Once this plan is set, take a few minutes each day to revisit the plan and to reflect on any successes for the day. Acknowledge any small failures but do not dwell on them. One of the goals is to replace negative thoughts with positive thoughts, so try to keep this activity as positive as possible.

Decide whether addiction is the biggest problem or if other problems in life are bigger. It may be that drinking is the one big problem in life. Some people drink to excess simply to drink to excess. They are not trying to cover up underlying problems or cope with life; they just drink too much because it is there to drink. These people will need to focus mainly on avoiding taking that next drink. But most people drink because they need to cope with life. These people will need to focus on ways to deal with the events and problems that crop up in everyday life that might cause the person to want to drink to excess again.

Remember that cravings can be controlled. Cravings are nothing more than a message the brain sends in response to a particular stimulus. Cravings do not last forever. Cravings will not kill a person, although it may feel like it at the time. And cravings cannot make anyone do anything they do not want to do. The choice is up to the individual.

Be ready to engage in a lifelong marathon. This is not a quick race. This will take forever, at least however long a person's forever is. An alcoholic who no longer drinks is recovering, always recovering. There is no cure to alcoholism.

There are outside forces that can help the recovering alcoholic on their way to recovery. Anyone who has ever had an addiction to alcohol and been successful in overcoming it will recommend taking advantage of one or more of these options to ensure the goal of sobriety is reached.

Of course, total abstinence must be observed. The recovering alcoholic must never drink again if they want to continue recovering. Even a drop of alcohol would be enough to trigger a relapse into mindless drinking. They must not have alcohol in the house or go to places alcohol will be served. This is especially important in the early days when will power is weak.

After leaving the rehabilitation center, there is always the possibility of returning. Especially in the beginning, some people feel the need for a refresher course, or they may feel as though they left the rehab facility before they were really ready. There is nothing wrong with this decision. The important thing is to do whatever needs to be done to help the addict recover.

Ongoing counseling is very important. The breakthroughs that happened while in rehab need to continue. More work needs to be done on triggers and cravings, and goals and achievements. There is no end to this journey; it is for life.

Never overlook the power of the buddy system. Having a buddy is crucial to recovery for the alcoholic. The buddy is the one person the addict can call who will always answer the phone, day or night. Living life as a sober person is difficult. A buddy is someone set up by the support group to be personally responsible for the sobriety of another person. This buddy must have shown that they have been sober for quite a while and are comfortable helping someone else to reach sobriety. This sponsor is responsible for doing everything they can to help another person not drink alcohol. They must always lead by example and encourage their buddy to attend as many meanings as possible. They guide their sponsee through the requirements of the group and what to do to be successful in sobriety. And, perhaps most importantly, they will answer the phone whenever their sponsee calls needing help in getting past that potentially fatal craving.

No discussion of alcohol addiction recovery would be complete without mentioning Alcoholics Anonymous (AA). AA was founded many years ago by two men who wanted a structured method to use to quit drinking. The program was based on using spiritual growth to achieve character development. One way to develop a good character was to refrain from drinking. They also developed the program of twelve steps that lead the practitioner to the ultimate goal of sobriety.

The policy of following the prescribed steps is crucial to success in AA. These steps are needed to ensure potential success. The addict must be able to accept that they have no power over alcohol but that it has much power over them. They need to believe in some sort of higher power of their choosing and to give their lives to the control of that higher power. They must be able to admit they have made mistakes and to own their mistakes. They must be willing to confront those people who have contributed to their addiction and to apologize to those they have hurt with their actions. And they must continually work through the process as the path to the goal changes because life changes.

The only definite requirement for joining an AA meeting is a fervent wish to live a sober life. AA accepts everyone whether rich or poor, regardless of race, creed, religion, origin, or anything else that might exclude someone from a group. In group meetings, only first names are used. This helps people feel that they can be totally open and honest about their past histories without giving up too much identifying information. And there is no age restriction for group meetings since alcoholism can strike at any age. One meeting a week is a bare minimum; people are encouraged to attend several meetings each week whenever possible. And everyone is encouraged to have a home meeting group where they go regularly, but it is an easy matter to find a group to join almost anywhere that the addict might be traveling for business or pleasure. The idea here is that there is always a group available for help. And it is during an AA meeting that one would be assigned a sponsor, that buddy who will answer the phone whenever they call.

Along with AA, there are the groups Al-anon and Alateen. Al-anon is a group for the friends and families of recovering alcoholics. Alcoholism is never a private disease. It affects everyone the alcoholic comes into contact with. Al-anon is a place these people can go to learn ways to cope, ways to help, and ways to forgive. Alateen does much the same thing, but it is specifically for young children and teens whose lives have been affected by someone who drinks, whether that person is currently in their lives or not. The alcoholic parent might still be present in the home. The alcoholic might be an absentee parent because of the alcoholism. Either way, the group will provide support when needed. Both groups offer the same type of sponsorship found in AA.

Setting oneself up for a good recovery is an important step on the road to recovery. The person who can leave alcohol addiction behind on their own is the rare person. Most people will need many levels of help before they can even begin to consider that sobriety might be a viable way of life. There is nothing wrong and everything right with being able to ask for help when it is needed. Remember this is a journey, and everyone needs help somewhere along the way. Just reach out and ask for it.

Chapter 9: The Role of Others in The Life of the Recovering Alcoholic

Addiction to any substance will affect everyone around the addict. People find it difficult to believe that anyone would prefer a drunken stupor to a life of sobriety. Keep in mind that alcoholism is a disease and must be treated as such. Someone who has a heart attack or a stroke will potentially have a long recovery period and will need support. The same is true of the alcoholic.

Every family group has a balance point. That is the point at which the family functions the best. This may not necessarily be a good function, but this is the way the family functions in this house. Every family is different, and the alcoholic's family is no exception to this rule.

The first problem the family might face after the alcoholic quits drinking is a shift in balance. The family life was settled around the care of the addict, and now that consideration has been removed. It can completely disrupt life as the family knows it and require a major rebalancing act to get back to normal. Keep in mind this is not the dictionary definition of normal but what is normal for the family.

Pretend the father is a raging alcoholic. The family has learned to walk on tiptoe when dad is home. No unnecessary noise is made in the house. Children tend to disappear, either to their rooms or somewhere outside, in order to avoid the wrath of dad. Mom might lie about problems the children might be having so that she will not incur dad's anger and the children will not suffer. When dad suddenly becomes sober and is no longer a raving lunatic the balance of the family has tilted. Dad might now want to have a relationship with the very children he has frightened so many times. Mom might not know how or when to share the children's activities with dad in the fear that he may go off the deep end again. The family will need to rebalance.

Suppose mom is the alcoholic. Mom is unable to do any of the things mommy usually does because she is always drinking or drunk. Dad and possible older children pick up the slack and do all the cooking, cleaning, and nurturing. Now suppose mom gets clean and comes home to resume her mommy life. She may be unable to because, for so long, she did none of these things. The children now turn to dad or older siblings for everything they need because mommy cannot be trusted to help them. The family will need to rebalance.

Whatever roles people play in the family, they need to expect that this new sobriety will cause changes in the family dynamic. In time these changes will be good ones that will serve to strengthen the family unit. Some adjustment will be needed to reach that point, but it is not impossible.

Chapter 10: The Dangers of Relapse

Long term sobriety is an achievable goal, with the right kind of work. Unfortunately, the level of support that is available in the early days is not the same level of support that will be available for the remainder of the addict's life. Eventually, it is understood that the person who is recovering has achieved a certain sense of self-worth and self-confidence and will be able to guide themselves, with minimal assistance, on their journey. This may not be the case for everyone. Some people enjoy a textbook recovery and rarely experience problems, but these people are very few and far between. Most people are quite human and become accustomed to a certain level of attention while they are recovering. When this attention is taken away, they may begin to falter.

Some specific signs signal that a relapse might be imminent. Cravings may begin to increase again. There may be thoughts of taking 'just one drink' just to get past a rough patch. The recovering alcoholic might feel abandoned or stuck in one place in their recovery. Feelings of depression and anxiety may return, worse than ever before. The addict may begin to deny his real feelings in favor of keeping the peace. They may begin to have an abnormal interest in other potentially harmful behaviors like gambling, overworking, overeating, or sexual experiencing. These new interests may become an addiction in themselves. These are mental reactions to a possible relapse that happen before the relapse occurs.

Next would be the physical reactions that will make the relapse more likely to happen. The physical part is more dangerous because it may involve an actual exposure to the very substance that caused a problem in the first place. This can include boredom with the current situation or fear that support may not be available when needed. Spending an inordinate amount of time talking about drinking is also a bad sign. There might be an actual feeling of physical pain that makes the addict think about drinking. There might be an increase in negative emotions like anxiety, sadness, and loneliness. Being around alcohol at this time would be particularly dangerous.

Again, the addict should never be afraid to ask for help. Just because the resources are no longer hovering does not mean that they are no longer available. The sponsor is still available anytime of the day or night. The members of the group are still there and ready to help. The counselor still has an office and is still ready to listen. When the addict regains some of their strength, this might be a good time to consider becoming a sponsor. Helping someone else along the path to sobriety is a wonderful way to renew one's own convictions in one's abilities.

Chapter 11: Pleasure Without Hangover

So the decision has been made, and the alcohol has been left behind. The addict has been through rehabilitation. The many counseling sessions have become the occasional visit. New friends have been made. Unfortunately, some old friends were lost along the way, but in the process of alcohol recovery that happens sometimes. The old hangouts are now off limits. The family is back together, and everyone seems to be enjoying the new dynamic. Work has never been better. What now?

Now is the time to learn to enjoy life without the bottle hanging around the neck like a big glass noose. Everything has now changed, most of it for the better, and it will continue to change for the positive as long as hard work and dedication are applied. Much of the early intense focus on remaining alcohol-free has relaxed and now it is time to get on with the business of enjoying life. But how?

There are a few truths about alcohol that no alcoholic will ever admit until after they quit drinking. Alcohol sneaks into a person's life under the guise of a friend, a helper. Alcohol will make everything better. Alcohol will make all the pain go away. Alcohol will make everything clear and sunny again. And in the beginning, it does just that. Drinking alcohol makes everything bigger and funnier. Life is so much better with alcohol.

Then alcohol begins to show its true colors, but the alcoholic cannot see these until they quit drinking. It is only then that they learn the dirty truth about alcohol.

Alcohol ends more fun than it starts. Constantly needing to find ways to work alcohol into the situation means missing out on a lot of fun. Think of all the parties never attended because alcohol was not offered. Think of all the children's plays and recitals missed or even gotten too late because of one more drink. The truth is that parties without alcohol are not dull; the dullness comes from the attendees who need alcohol to liven up and cannot function if it is not present.

Alcohol will steal from anyone it finds to steal from. Alcohol does not care. Alcohol will ruin a person's health. The longer someone drinks the more health problems they will experience. And some of these problems have no cure when they get to their worst stage: think heart attack, stroke, and a dead liver. Alcohol steals relationships and makes the alcoholic a lonely person. Alcohol steal time that could better be spent on anything else but is now lost forever. And alcohol steals money because alcohol in excess is very expensive.

If possible, the recovering alcoholic should watch other sober people in the process of getting drunk. They will be able to see their friends turn into bleary-eyed uncoordinated strangers. They will laugh at things that are not really funny. They will insist they are having a wonderful time when the smile on their faces does not reach their eyes. And tomorrow morning they will wake up with dry mouth and a hangover while trying to recall what really happened last night.

The real truth is that embracing sobriety is not so much about the end of a life and more about the beginning. Certainly, the party life must be left behind. But so much more of life is now open for the taking that it can sometimes feel unbelievable.

People who have started on a life of sobriety now have time to learn who they are and what they want out of life. There is no longer the consideration of needing a drink, or several, to be able to function. Now they can decide what they want out of all areas of life. Is the addict holding onto a particular job they do not like simply because the employer put up with him when he was drinking? If so it might be time for a career change. While it is nice if an employer stuck behind a person, that bond will not hold two people together forever. Decide what type of career is best and make a change if the time feels right.

Now is the time to enjoy family outings. Think of all the school plays, recitals, family picnics, holiday dinners, birthdays, that were missed because either alcohol was not being served or the addict was already too drunk to participate. There is no alcohol standing in the way anymore. Enjoy the family and spend some time mending fences. It will be well worth the work.

Did any hobbies get left behind in the search for the next drink? Or were some never attempted because they might interfere with drinking? Now is the time to pick up the brush and easel that has been collecting dust in the attic. That project car in the garage, the one that has been waiting under a tarp for years, could be the perfect vessel for reconnecting with the kids. Maybe the community center has been offering a pottery class for years that directly interfered with happy hour. Well, alcohol is now out of the picture, and now it is time to find a hobby or two to enrich life.

If the most horrible thing happened and late night drinking and driving resulted in the loss of a license and driving privileges, now is the time to work on getting them back. An approved alcohol awareness program is usually a requirement to regain a lost license. Someone already on the road to sobriety has already taken the necessary steps to becoming a sober driver and the courts like that. Get the license back and get out in the world again.

Sobriety will not always be easy. Never drinking again will sometimes be the hardest decision ever made. Twenty years in the clear might pass, and one horrible event might prompt a craving for a drink. This is a life-long journey that is worth so much to every area of life that it makes no sense not to start on the path. With hard work and dedication, the goal of sobriety can be reached.